Prayer 101

Foundation for Faith and Formation

THERESA A. JONES

Liguori

Imprimi Potest: Stephen T. Rehrauer, CSsR, Provincial
Denver Province, the Redemptorists

Imprimatur: "In accordance with CIC 827, permission to publish has been granted on October 20, 2021, by the Most Reverend Mark S. Rivituso, Auxiliary Bishop, Archdiocese of St. Louis. Permission to publish is an indication that nothing contrary to Church teaching is contained in this work. It does not imply any endorsement of the opinions expressed in the publication; nor is any liability assumed by this permission."

Published by Liguori Publications, Liguori, Missouri 63057
Liguori Publications, a nonprofit corporation, is an apostolate of the Redemptorists (Redemptorists.com).

Phone: 800-325-9521 *Web:* Liguori.org

Prayer 101: Foundation for Faith and Formation
Copyright © 2022 Theresa A. Jones
ISBN 978-0-7648-2859-1
Library of Congress Control number: 2021950516

Unless noted otherwise, Scripture texts herein are from the *New American Bible, revised edition* © 2010, 1991, 1986, 1970 Confraternity of Christian Doctrine, Washington, DC, and are used with the permission of the copyright owner. All Rights Reserved. No part of the *New American Bible* may be reproduced in any form without permission in writing from the copyright owner.

Excerpts from the English translation of the *Catechism of the Catholic Church* for use in the United States of America © 1997, United States Catholic Conference, Inc.

Excerpts from Vatican documents used with permission.
Copyright © 2022 *Libreria Editrice Vaticana*

Cover design: John Krus
Cover photo: Love You Stock/Shutterstock

Printed in the United States of America
26 25 24 23 22 / 5 4 3 2 1
First Edition

Dedication

I dedicate this book to my incredible son, Jeremy.

Your adventurous spirit certainly kept me on my knees!

I am so grateful for our journey together through the years.

I will love you forever!

May you rest in peace.

ACKNOWLEDGMENTS

This book is a product of a lifetime of living, loving, and praying. The desire of my heart has been to, in some way, help others know and love God, who first loves all of us. This desire, the inspiration for this book, has been nourished by almost everyone I've known. I have been so blessed to have been surrounded by people who know and love God and wish to share him with others. For all of you, I am so grateful for the ways you have helped create this book, but also for the example you have provided for me to be a vessel of love to our hurting world.

More specifically I want to thank my husband, Keith, who, through the journey of writing this book, has been by my side, loving, supporting, and encouraging me through long hours, days, weeks, and months. You are such a blessing in my life!

I owe a debt of gratitude to all my friends who encouraged me, but especially those I pressed into service and who lovingly responded as readers and proofreaders: Georgia Costalas, Ginny Brown, Karen DeCrosta, and Fr. Steve Stavoy.

To my Carmelite family, from your examples of lives lived for God, to years of formal formation on prayer and the contemplative life, to many years of spiritual direction, I am so grateful—especially Rose Mary Lancelotti, TOC; and Fr. Paul DeNault, OCarm.

This book started as a desire to offer a course on prayer while I was an adjunct professor at Mount Saint Mary College. My department chair, Dr. Robert Miller, encouraged me to create and offer the course. Thank you for believing in me!

Thank you also to Tom Heine, my developmental editor, and all the staff at Liguori Publications who have answered all my questions and helped me every step of the way.

Thank you most of all to God, who has called and empowered me to write this simple book, allowing me to work for his honor and glory!

Laudem Gloriae
Praise of Glory

Contents

Introduction

Meet Sally, a kind, compassionate, Catholic mom. While shopping for her family, she bumps into Karen at the supermarket. They exchange greetings, and then Karen talks about the struggles she is having with her young daughter, Beth. Apparently, Beth is starting to run with a bad crowd, becoming very private, and putting up a big fuss when it's time to go to Sunday Mass. Sally, a compassionate friend, feels for Karen's struggle and wants to help. She offers to pray for her friend. On her way home she questions herself: *I said I'd pray for Karen, but what does that mean? When I was a child, I know my mother would sometimes pray a rosary for her friend. I certainly don't remember how to do that or have time for it. What should I do to pray for Karen? What are my options?*

Does this sound familiar? If so, you are in the right place. It's interesting how the subject of eternity, specifically heaven and hell, is rarely discussed. People have conversations about careers, investments, retirement savings, and the like, but these only help us during our time on earth. Yet prayer, a topic that impacts eternity, often gets left by the wayside. Why? Most people are very private about their prayer life and shy away from discussing it. It is almost as if, as one author put it, we have inherited a "bashfulness gene" when it comes to prayer. One reason is that while many people love and believe in God—perhaps going so far as to attend Bible studies, learn about saints, or watch religious videos—many don't have a good vocabulary to discuss prayer. They have no common language and very little education on this crucial aspect of our life with God, meaning the Father, the Son, and the Holy Spirit. Unfortunately, the average person reflects a third- or fourth-grade understanding of prayer. As adults we have grown in our understanding of so much in the world—relationships, technology, health, even the Church and God—but very little on prayer. A lucky few have been fortunate to have good mentors in developing a prayer life—parents, parish priests, religious sisters or brothers. Others have taken it upon themselves to seek out information on prayer. There are many books on prayer. Most can give you a how-to on praying in one style or another. These can be helpful but often assume an understanding of the foundations of what prayer is.

Prayer 101, part of Liguori Publications' series of *101* books, will examine what it means to pray—for your own affairs, your kids, your friends, your country, anything and anyone. It begins by defining prayer, the reasons people pray, and identifying some basic divisions in prayer types and forms. The rest of the book will examine some common divisions and give examples. My hope is to help you develop a vocabulary for discussing prayer while building a framework to understand different types of prayer. With this framework, I hope you will be able to easily find ways to pray that suit you, enabling you to develop a stronger relationship with our loving God, who continually calls out to each of us to spend time with him in prayer.

THERESA A. JONES
LAKE ARIEL, PENNSYLVANIA

CHAPTER 1

What Is Prayer?

At every time and in every place, God draws near to
each human person.

CATECHISM OF THE CATHOLIC CHURCH, 1

What is prayer? At first glance it appears to be a simple question. One of the problems is that there is not one comprehensive definition that can truly encompass the truth of what prayer is. While teaching at a small college in New York, I asked some of my students how they would define prayer. Responses included: "When I talk to God." "What I do when I go to church." "Connecting with Jesus." "Saying a rosary." It seemed there were as many answers as there were respondents. Prayer is a very personal thing.

Oxford Languages' dictionary defines prayer as "a solemn request for help or expression of thanks addressed to God or an object of worship," "an earnest wish or hope," and "a set order of words used in praying." Saint Augustine of Hippo (354–430), a bishop, states prayer is "a turning of the heart to God." Saint Thérèse of Lisieux (1873–97), a Carmelite nun, says it is "a surge of the heart; it is a simple look turned toward heaven." Fr. Thomas H. Green, SJ (1932–2009), author of many books on prayer, including *Opening to God* and *Experiencing God*, defines it as "a personal encounter with God in love." Fr. Martin Pable, OFM Cap (1931–2020), author of *Prayer: A Practical Guide*, states prayer is "any act whereby we consciously attend to the presence of God within us or around us." The *Catechism of the Catholic Church* defines it as "the raising of one's mind and heart to God" (*CCC* 2559). Further in the *Catechism,* the definition is extended to include the first steps of prayer being about connection:

> God calls man first. Man may forget his Creator or hide far from his face; he may run after idols or accuse the deity of having abandoned him; yet the living and true God tirelessly calls each person to that mysterious encounter known as prayer. In prayer, the faithful God's initiative of love always comes first; our own first step is always a response. As God gradually reveals himself and reveals man to himself, prayer appears as a reciprocal call, a covenant drama. Through words and actions, this drama engages the heart. It unfolds throughout the whole history of salvation (*CCC* 2567).

God first calls man. Bishop Robert Barron, auxiliary bishop of the Archdiocese of Los Angeles and a prominent Catholic podcaster, in his YouTube video "Bishop Barron on Prayer," says that "biblical religion is not primarily our quest for God. It is God's quest for us. So, once we see the primacy of grace, prayer is God's addressing us." Quoting Dominican theologian Herbert McCabe, Bishop Barron goes on to say if there is anything in our prayer that is good, true, and right, that is a sign the Holy Spirit is already praying in us.

Prayer, then, is our response to the work of the Holy Spirit. Therefore, prayer is a positive response rather than a direct action on our part. If a mother bakes cookies and then offers one to a child, we would understand that the receiving of that cookie is the child's response to the mother's action. Prayer is my "child" response to God, Father. "God proves his love for us in that while we still were sinners Christ died for us" (Romans

5:8). God takes the first step, we respond. Our prayer is always a response to God's outstretched arms. He tirelessly calls each person to prayer. "The desire for God is written in the human heart, because man is created by God and for God; and God never ceases to draw man to himself" (*CCC* 27).

We are hard-wired, so to speak, to be drawn to God. While humanity searches for the sense of fulfillment that can only be found in God, often we search for it in everything but God—money, power, fame. If God is the initiator, then prayer can be understood more as an opening of the mind and heart to God. God is already working to draw us in. We just need to be open to his efforts. For this book I will be using this definition of prayer: an opening of the mind and heart to God. In so doing, I recognize what we do as the response to God's action. Lifting, turning, worshiping, and other responses all suggest we are the ones initiating the prayer. But opening up to receive more clearly shows God as the initiator. We simply respond.

WHY DO WE PRAY?

In ancient times, pagans who believed in other gods would pray to keep the gods from getting angry. If they kept their gods happy, they believed they would have fertile crops and the weather would be favorable. Their prayers were actions based on fear and their hopes of getting their own needs met. One might say their "prayers" were completely self-focused.

So as Christians, why do we pray? I turned again to my students and asked them to interview their peers and family to find why they pray. Those questioned and many others I've spoken with say people generally pray to make a request. Why do we turn to God to ask for things like healing for a friend or relative, to get a job, to get things we desire? Aren't we then like the pagans? I hope not. Christians strive to have a personal relationship with the one true God and recognize he is omnipresent (always present), omniscient (all-knowing), omnipotent (all-powerful), and omnibenevolent (all-good and loving). God desires only our good and cares about everything that involves each of us and all of creation. God, through Scripture, tells us directly to ask: "Ask and it will be given to you; seek and you will find; knock and the door will be opened to you" (Matthew 7:7). This is what we do. Further commenting on prayer, Pope Francis says, "You pray for the hungry. Then you feed them. That's how prayer works."

If we ask to receive, then we hope God grants our request. If I needed a thousand dollars, would I ask my poor, elderly neighbor if he could spot me a grand? Why would I? I would not expect him to be able to do it—I wouldn't even bother to ask. On the other hand, if I asked my wealthy uncle to lend me a thousand, I'd be asking with an expectation my request could be filled. And so it is with God. He is able to provide the help we seek. So, we ask with an open, hopeful, and expectant heart, having faith that God can and desires to do so.

If I ask the man in front of me in line at the supermarket to hand me a copy of a magazine, have I opened my heart to him? Probably not. If I ask my husband to hold me after receiving some bad news, does that involve opening my heart? Yes. What is the difference? One involves relationship and love, a level of trust, and a deep desire for the welfare and good of the other. Asking a guy at the supermarket to hand me a periodical does not. God deeply, truly, and eternally desires the best for each of us. So, as we make our requests known to God, our definition reminds us to open our mind and heart to God, to his love, to his presence.

SCRIPTURE TELLS US SO

God has made it known—even requested—that we connect with him, walk with him, sing his praises. Where do we find this direction from God? In sacred Scripture, his written word, Jesus taught us in the prayer we call the Our Father to ask for "our daily bread." In John's Gospel, Jesus says, "Amen, amen, I say to you, whatever you ask the Father in my name he will give you" (John 16:23). God is all-knowing, yet he implores us to ask for our needs. By doing this we recognize our dependence on him. "We are creatures who are not our own beginning, not the masters of adversity, not our own last end. We are sinners who as Christians know that we have turned away from our Father. Our petition is already a turning back to him" (*CCC* 2629). We turn back to God, the source of all that is true and beautiful. If left to our own devices, we choose darkness, but with God we can choose life.

In Genesis, we see Adam and Eve walk and talk with God. It appears to be a natural, intimate relationship, until their fall from grace when sin and disobedience enter the scene. The Fall creates a rift between people and God that humanity in its sinfulness cannot fix. The rest of the Scriptures are about restoring that once-perfect, intimate, and trusting relationship with God. To restore it, God continually reaches out to his people. The Noah's Ark story illustrates this. After the Fall, humanity turns from God, and corruption becomes normal. God wants to hit the reset button on creation by sending a flood. He finds one righteous man, Noah, and calls him to build an ark to save God's creation. Could God have addressed the problem alone? Yes, but he chooses to work with Noah. By working together as God did with Noah, the trust and intimacy between God and people begins to be restored. If God had acted alone, there would have been no progress on this all-important restoration.

Fast-forward to the time of Abraham. God once again calls to man to work with him to advance his efforts in restoring this relationship. Abram, as he was originally called, hears God calling to him in the desert "to a land that I will show you" (Genesis 12:1). God tells Abraham he will bless him and make of him a great nation. God calls Abraham and his descendants to be a people particularly his own, "the apple of his eye" (Deuteronomy 32:10). Through these people, God will show humanity his goodness, strength, and power. The goal is to bring all people into relationship with himself.

The Book of Psalms is filled with God's people calling out to him for help in their time of need—in sickness, danger, poverty, even depression.

> Incline your ear, LORD, and answer me,
> for I am poor and oppressed.
> Preserve my life, for I am devoted;
> save your servant who trusts in you.
>
> PSALM 86:1–2

> The LORD is my light and my salvation;
> whom should I fear?
> The LORD is my life's refuge;
> of whom should I be afraid?
> ...Though an army encamp against me,
> my heart does not fear;
> Though war be waged against me, even then do I trust.
> One thing I ask of the LORD;
> this I seek:

To dwell in the LORD's house
all the days of my life,
To gaze on the LORD's beauty,
to visit his temple.
For God will hide me in his shelter
in time of trouble,
he will conceal me in the cover of his tent;
and set me high upon a rock.

PSALM 27:1, 3–5

God's people are told many times to call to him; to ponder, trust, and dwell with him. Each instance is a time of prayer, a connection with God that involves trust and an open heart. Prayer is such a central topic in Scripture that the word *pray* appears 454 times, almost as many times as the word *love* (569).

In the Scriptures, God repeatedly called his people to pray, as he continues to call us today. This connection with God can take many different forms—seeking, talking, listening, meditating, crying out, and interceding, as just a few examples. Not only are there multiple forms for prayer, but there are also many ways of understanding these particular words and of putting them into practice. One might refer to meditation as mulling over the words of Scripture while another may use that word to describe silent prayer. This can be confusing. I do not seek to give absolute definitions for the vocabulary of prayer, but I do seek to offer a way to organize these words that may simplify our understanding of the topic. In setting up a "working vocabulary," I have divided prayer into different modes, types, and forms. I will describe them as we move along. In the next chapter, explore with me some common traditional prayers.

REFLECTION QUESTIONS

1. *In the list of definitions of prayer, does one resonate with
    you more than the others? How does this definition connect
    with your understanding of who God is?*

2. *What is our desire to pray a sign of? Why?*

3. *Do you pray? If so, what are some reasons you choose to
    pray? Do you feel comfortable about the way you pray?*

4. *Humanity's relationship with God was broken by the Fall
    of Adam and Eve. What, then, is the purpose of all that
    follows, both in Scripture and in all of history since the
    Fall?*

CHAPTER 2

Traditional Prayers

You met Sally in the introduction. She sought ways to pray for a friend. She knows the Our Father and the Creed, since they are said at Mass weekly. They are examples of traditional prayers—written by others, approved by the Church, and handed down through the generations. Sally can use these prayers to pray for her friend. Traditional prayers can be prayed alone or with others, and they follow a predetermined set of words. Before the Second Vatican Council (Vatican II) in the 1960s, the prayers of most Catholics consisted of the rosary, ones prayed at Mass, and other traditional prayers. My parents and others believed these to be all there was to prayer.

PRIMARY PRAYERS

Traditional prayers are directly from or rooted in the truths found in the sacred Scriptures. The Our Father, for example, the most popular and well-known traditional prayer, was given to us by Jesus in the Gospel of Luke and at the Sermon on the Mount in Matthew. The Lord's disciples asked Jesus to teach them how to pray (see Luke 11:1–4). He responded by teaching them the Our Father. The words vary from Gospel to Gospel, but the truths do not.

Our Father in heaven,
hallowed be your name,
your kingdom come,
your will be done,
on earth as in heaven.
Give us today our daily bread;
and forgive us our debts,
as we forgive our debtors;
and do not subject us to the final test,
but deliver us from the evil one.

MATTHEW 6:9–13

Catholics learn that the Our Father "is truly the summary of the whole gospel" (*CCC* 2761). All that Jesus strives to teach us can be found in the seven petitions of the prayer he taught his disciples. After the greeting, three petitions recognize the truths of God: hallowed be thy name, thy kingdom come, and thy will be done. God is to be praised, he is the king of creation, and his will for the world is the supreme good over all else. The next petitions are based on our needs: give us, forgive us, lead us, and deliver us. These cover all the truths in the Gospels.

Other traditional prayers include the Hail Mary, the Glory Be (Doxology), the Creed, the Sign of the Cross, Grace Before Meals, and the Angel of God, all of which are in Appendix A, with the approved wording of the US Conference of Catholic Bishops. Many of the words and all the truths of the Hail Mary are found in Scripture. "Hail Mary, full of grace, the Lord is with thee" (Luke 1:28), is when the angel Gabriel greets Mary at the annunciation. In Luke 1:42, Mary's cousin Elizabeth greets her and says, "Most blessed are you among women, and blessed is the fruit of your womb." Elizabeth, in the next verse, conveys that Mary is the Mother of God: "And how does this happen to me that the mother of my Lord should come to me?"

Throughout the Bible we see examples of one person praying for another person or group of people (Exodus 32:30–33, 1 Chronicles 21:17, James 5:14–16). This is called *intercession*. In the New Testament, Jesus tells his disciples to go out and pray with the lame and those in bondage that they may be healed. This is done through praying for others. James 5:16 says, "Pray for one another." From these and many other examples we get the wording, "Pray for us sinners, now and at the hour of our death." While the exact words of the Hail Mary are not found in the Scripture the way the Our Father is, the truths in Scripture are clearly the basis of this traditional prayer.

The Sign of the Cross, also a traditional prayer is the most common of Catholic prayers. Though it often precedes a prayer, it can also be used as a standalone prayer. When I am in an airplane as it gains speed taxiing down the runway, I always bless myself with the sign of the cross. It's common to see athletes do this as they step up to bat or attempt a field goal. Of course, viewers may wonder if the gesture comes from a heart open to God—if even briefly. If so, it is prayer. If not, it could be no more than a superstitious good-luck charm. Only the person making the gesture knows the truth.

When a person truly prays this simple sign, he or she is affirming belief in the Trinity: Father, Son, and Holy Spirit. It is also a reminder of our Lord's triumph over sin and death through his mighty cross. Through this profession of faith, when prayed with a heart open to God, it becomes a vessel of God's grace. Scripture says we are to pray in the name of Jesus (see John 14:13). Jesus prayed in the name of the Father, and the love shared between Father and Son is the Holy Spirit. When a person begins and ends her or his prayer with the sign of the cross, that person is praying in Jesus' name as Scripture directs. The actions of the sign of the cross affirm the core of our beliefs as Christians—the Trinity's existence and Jesus' crucifixion.

Evidence of the use of this sign can be seen in the third century when Tertullian, an early Christian theologian, wrote, "At every forward step and movement, at every going in and out, when we put on our clothes and shoes, when we bathe, when we sit at table, when we light the lamps, on couch, on seat, in all the ordinary actions of daily life, we trace upon the forehead the sign."

The Creed is derived from the Latin *credo*, meaning, "I believe." It is a summary or statement of belief and a traditional prayer. It is sometimes referred to as a mini-Bible. When my son was small, we visited Florida. While there, he got a toy that included directions to place it in water. When he allowed it to soak overnight, the next morning he discovered a rubbery alligator more than 500 percent the size of the original capsule. He was very excited. The Creed is like that. Each line, each carefully chosen word, declares profound truths that, when examined, seems to "grow" hundreds or even thousands of times greater and deeper.

Like the Trinity, the Creed can be understood in three parts. The first part focuses on the Creator of all, the Father. The second part focuses on the divine Son. The third part regards belief in the Holy Spirit. The earliest known Christian creed is the Apostles' Creed. It was used in teaching new believers the foundations of the faith.

"From the beginning, the apostolic Church expressed and handed on the faith in brief normative formula for all. But already...early on, the Church also wanted to convey the essential elements of the faith into organic and articulated summaries, intended especially for candidates for baptism" (*CCC* 186).

The Creed basically has been used for three main purposes: confession, teaching, and as a rule of faith. Those who have wanted to enter the Church have confessed their belief in the truth of these proclamations. For those already baptized in the

Church, the Creed has been a guide for teaching the faith. Today, section one of the *Catechism* employs the Creed to explain the elements of the Catholic faith. It also has been used as a rule of faith to guard against heresies—teachings opposed to the official teachings of the Catholic Church.

A heresy on the nature of Jesus called Arianism, fostered in the fourth century, declared that Jesus was fully human but not divine. At the First Council of Nicaea in the year 325, the Apostles' Creed was expanded to clarify the Church's teaching that Jesus is fully man and fully God. The "I believe in Jesus Christ, his only Son, our Lord" of the Apostles' Creed was expanded in the Nicene Creed to state in part:

> I believe in one Lord Jesus Christ,
> the Only Begotten Son of God,
> born of the Father before all ages.
> God from God, Light from Light,
> true God from true God,
> begotten, not made, consubstantial with the Father;
> through him all things were made.
> For us men and for our salvation
> he came down from heaven....

Other creeds written through the centuries have addressed other heresies, but only the Apostles' and Nicene Creeds hold prominent places in our life in the Church. The Apostles' Creed is recited during the praying of the rosary and sometimes during the Mass. The Nicene Creed is sometimes prayed during Mass. A Creed clearly states to the world what we believe. And we can reasonably trust that those we gather with on Sunday share the beliefs we state in the Creed. Part one of the *Catechism* has more on the Creed.

DEVOTIONAL PRAYERS

Litanies have been part of the Church's treasury of traditional prayers since at least the third century. *Litany* comes from the Greek *litaneia*, meaning "entreaty or request." A litany is basically structured as a series of invocations followed by the same repeated response. Generally a leader, often a priest, reads the request and the people answer with the responses. Litanies are typically used in processions, to help our growth in particular virtues, as a form of request, or for visiting the sick and the dying. Litanies are frequently arranged around a sacred theme or person: the Litany of Humility, the Litany of St. Thérèse, or the Litany for a Happy Death, to name a few.

From the Litany of the Saints

Holy Mary,	pray for us.
Holy Mother of God,	pray for us
Holy Virgin of Virgins,	pray for us.
St. Michael,	pray for us.
St. Gabriel,	pray for us.

The earliest known litanies are the Litany of Loreto and the Litany of the Saints. By the 1600s, as many as eighty litanies were in use. To prevent litanies that may not conform to Catholic doctrine, Pope Clement VIII restricted the use of litanies in liturgical settings. Only five litanies have been approved for liturgical use: the Sacred Heart, the Precious Blood, the Saints, the Blessed Virgin Mary (also known as the Litany of Loreto), and the Litany of St. Joseph. The Litany of Saints is often used during the Easter Vigil and at baptisms. Other litanies may be used individually or by groups in private, nonliturgical settings.

In the Old Testament, particularly in the Psalms, one can

find prayers or songs that follow a similar format. Psalm 136 has the repeated response of "for his mercy endures forever." In the Book of Daniel, when three young men were put in a fiery furnace for refusing to pray to a foreign god, they responded, "Praise and exalt him above all forever" (see Daniel 3:57–87). In the Mass, this form of responsorial prayer is found in the Responsorial Psalm and the Prayer of the Faithful. During the Responsorial Psalm, the lector or a vocalist reads or sings the psalm, and all respond. In the Prayer of the Faithful, a priest or deacon states the petition and the congregants respond, "Lord, hear our prayer" or something similar.

The Stations of the Cross (also known as the Way of the Cross) is a traditional prayer that commemorates Jesus' passion and death. Early Christians would travel to Jerusalem and retrace the final journey of Jesus to Calvary, focusing on fourteen stops along the way. Later, for the many who wanted to pass along the same route but could not make the trip to Jerusalem, a practice developed of meditating on the fourteen stops, or stations. The stations are set in the Church's Tradition, but each stop may include a meditation that can vary, according to the US Conference of Catholic Bishops (USCCB). Depictions of these stations may be found in most Catholic churches. The Stations of the Cross is generally prayed during Lent but can be prayed at any time. Some frequently used versions include stations by Sts. Alphonsus Liguori and Francis of Assisi.

A *novena* (Latin for "nine") is a series of prayers that are often prewritten and said over the course of nine days. It can be said alone or with a group. Nine days became traditional because Jesus told his disciples at his ascension to wait and pray for the Holy Spirit to descend upon them, and we believe the Holy Spirit descended on the ninth day. A novena is prayed for a special request, especially a healing or for a deceased loved one or in preparation for a feast day such as Christmas, the annunciation, and the feast of St. Thérèse. The novena requests special graces or favors through the intercession of the Virgin Mary or the saints. For example, each year, starting on July 8, many pray the novena to Our Lady of Mount Carmel, whose feast is celebrated July 16. Some novenas comprise the same prayer or set of prayers, prayed on each of the nine days. Others have different prayers for each day, but all have the same theme. If you wish, you may choose your own prayers to offer on each of the nine days. Novenas for the Holy Spirit, the Holy Souls in Purgatory, Our Lady of Perpetual Help, Our Lady of Mount Carmel, and the Little Flower are some of the more common ones. Our friend Sally could choose to offer a novena to the Blessed Mother or some other saint for her friend.

Some novenas and other pious acts have an indulgence attached to them, from the Latin *indulgentia*, meaning "to be kind or tender." Catholics understand an indulgence "is the remission before God of the temporal punishment due to sins whose guilt has already been forgiven" (*CCC* 1471).

"A further distinction is made between perpetual indulgences, which may be gained at any time, and temporary, which are available on certain days only, or within certain periods," writes William Kent in *The Catholic Encyclopedia*. For example, during the 2016 Year of Mercy, temporary indulgences were attached to walking through a particular doorway of certain churches. The more important distinction in indulgences is between plenary and partial indulgences.

> [A plenary indulgence means] the remission of the entire temporal punishment due to sin so no further expiation is required in *purgatory* (emphasis mine). A partial indulgence commutes only a certain portion of the penalty; and this portion is determined in accordance with the penitential discipline of the early Church. To say that an

indulgence of so many days or years is granted means that it cancels an amount of purgatorial punishment equivalent to that which would have been remitted, in the sight of God, by the performance of so many days or years of the ancient canonical penance. Here, evidently, the reckoning makes no claim to absolute exactness; it has only a relative value.

WILLIAM KENT, *THE CATHOLIC ENCYCLOPEDIA*

Since it is impossible to determine specific remissions and was widely misunderstood, this numbering was done away with. The Church has not ceased indulgences, though. They are important for our growth in holiness as well as those of our loved ones. Frequently plenary indulgences are used for our deceased loved ones to shorten their time in purgatory. They need our prayers, as they can make no progress on their own.

The rosary is a set of traditional prayers prayed in a predetermined format to honor the Blessed Virgin Mary while encouraging the prayer to meditate on the life of Christ. *Rosary* is based on the Latin for "garland of roses," with the rose symbolizing the Mother of Jesus. The rosary is a biblical prayer. Saint John Paul II's apostolic letter on the Most Holy Rosary (*Rosarium Virginis Mariae*) stated that while it is clearly "Marian in character, [it] is at heart, a Christocentric prayer." The US bishops state "the repetition in the rosary is meant to lead one into restful and contemplative prayer related to each mystery. The gentle repetition of the words helps one to enter the silence of their hearts, where Christ's spirit dwells. The rosary can be said privately or with a group." The simple, rhythmic nature of the rosary combined with the meditative focus on the Gospels attract many—adults, teens, and children—to this prayer form. Pope Francis offers encouragement: "Make use of this powerful instrument, the prayer of the Holy Rosary, because it brings peace to hearts, to families, the Church and the World," he said. Chapter six features more on the rosary and praying with Mary.

Traditional prayers are often recited in a repetitive way, either daily or one after another, as in the rosary. This repetition is soothing, minimizing struggles with prayer, and can help center the mind and spirit. Repetitive prayer has a long tradition in Judeo-Christian history. The Jewish people of the Old Testament and today pray the psalms day and night, as do many Christians. On certain days they pray certain psalms. This applied to Jesus himself, a faithful Jew who followed the prayer traditions of his time.

> Protestants often claim that to repeat a prayer is of no benefit, yet Christ himself whom we should all imitate taught us to pray in such a manner as he himself prayed repeating the same words. We see this at Gethsemane, where he (Jesus) says, "My Father, if it is possible, let this cup pass from me; yet, not as I will, but as you will" (Matthew 26:36–44)...[Later in this passage] we read that Christ went away praying for the "third time, saying the same thing."...For he even spoke to his people saying, "These people honor me with their lips, but their hearts are far from me" (Matthew 15:8). From this we know that God knows our hearts and he seeks to converse with our hearts (our eternal souls) in prayer."
>
> "THE HOLY ROSARY"
> CATHOLICAPOLOGETICS.INFO/
> APOLOGETICS/GENERAL/HOLYRSRY.HTM

Some say the repetition causes them to slip into saying words with a wandering mind. It might help to remember two things: First, whenever praying, always strive to open your heart and mind to God. An open heart and mind transforms plain words into prayer. I can repeat an eloquent prayer thousands of times, but if I fail to do so with a heart open to God, I'm like a "clashing cymbal" (1 Corinthians 13:1). Rambled words with no intent to connect with God is not prayer. "In praying, do not babble like the pagans, who think that they will be heard because of their many words," Jesus says (Matthew 6:7). Also, when we strive to focus on God in prayer, God sees that effort and blesses it. Remember, prayer is about connecting with God.

DISTRACTIONS IN PRAYER

Distractions are common in prayer, especially with traditional prayers. There are ways to manage some of these distractions. First, remember you are in God's holy presence. If we keep this in mind, we are less likely to be distracted and feel we are speaking into an empty void. When distractions come and your mind wanders, are you still sitting or kneeling with your heart open to God and with the intent to pray? If so, your will is to pray; therefore, you are still connecting with God. Whenever your mind wanders, you can choose to give up on prayer or return to opening your heart to God. Each time you choose to stay with God in prayer, you are choosing God.

Distractions are part of the human condition, but you can do things to minimize them. Try having a consistent time for prayer. Your mind and body are programmed for schedules. The sun rises and sets on a cycle, the months come and go on a cycle. Experts say that going to sleep and rising at the same time each day benefits our well-being. Along this same line, when we create a habit of praying at the same time each day, our mind and body learn to anticipate it and can prepare for settling down and focusing on God.

Where you pray can also be important. If you have a consistent place where you are comfortable, and if you have prayer aids (a Bible, image, devotional, or rosary, for example), you are less likely to be distracted. Sleep experts say that using your bed solely for sleep and physical intimacy programs your body to associate the bed with those activities. The same can be said for a prayer space. Choosing to pray at the kitchen table while others prepare for the day—getting coffee, making breakfast, and watching the news—is not conducive to distraction-free prayer time. Having a prayer time and place is helpful in reducing distractions, but it will not eliminate them. When they come, it is best not to get agitated. Just focus on God and open your heart again to his presence and peace.

REFLECTION QUESTIONS

1. *Traditional prayers are based on fundamental truths. Examine the Glory Be. What foundational truths do you see?*

2. *Were you taught traditional prayers while growing up? If so, what truths did these specific prayers teach you?*

3. *What are the major differences between the Apostles' Creed and Nicene Creed?*

4. *How did the practice of the Stations of the Cross begin? Have you noticed them on your Church walls? Do they help you reflect?*

5. *The souls in purgatory need our help to pass through to the fullness of God's presence. What can you do to help them on their journey?*

6. *What benefits do you see in using traditional prayers when praying? What problems might arise in using only traditional prayers in your prayer life?*

CHAPTER 3

Conversational Prayers

I n the first chapter, we looked at some traditional prayers—ones written by others and approved by the Church. Traditional prayers are the staple for most Catholics worldwide. They allow us to pray with one voice, giving unity. Using traditional prayers, some find the connection with God they are seeking. That is completely fine. Others are drawn to look for something more personalized. This is not to suggest one method is better than another. However, one format may fit us better during one time in our life than another. Our prayer journey is about connection and relationship with God. This relationship has the potential to live, breathe, and grow as all relationships do. This does not necessarily mean you should change your prayer format, as God is not limited by any format.

Earlier I asked if there are drawbacks to traditional prayers. One may include difficulty in speaking to God from your heart. When we talk with our friends, we don't use formal language. In a dating relationship, nothing beats hearing how the person you are dating feels straight from the lips. Another possible hurdle is that the words of the prayer may go too far for where you are in your relationship with God. A prayer might say, "I love you God with every fiber of my being." While this is a wonderful sentiment, if you are not quite there, try, "I want to love you with every fiber of my being." "I want to" may fit people who aren't quite "there."

This is where conversational prayer comes in. Conversational prayer in its basic form is speaking to God from your heart. It could be as simple as, "Oh God, let me get to work on time." God likes to hear what is on your heart and mind directly from you. It makes the prayer more personal.

Most people are familiar with this style. In fact, when I questioned students on a college campus, 90 percent said their prayer style is conversational. After I explained what conversational prayer is about, some who initially said they don't pray at all realize they do indeed pray this way.

Conversational prayer reminds me of *Fiddler on the Roof*, the classic theatrical musical and movie. It is about a Jewish man, Tevye, trying to maintain his family's religion and culture in early-1900s Russia. Tevye is a man of God who strives to follow the Lord's ways even when life is difficult and the Lord's plan is unclear. In his relationship with God, Tevye the milkman talks conversationally with God as he walks along his dairy route, sometimes asking for help, at times thanking him, and at other times complaining, like this:

> Dear God, was that necessary? Did you have to make him (my horse) lame just before the Sabbath? That wasn't nice. It's enough you pick on me. Bless me with five daughters, a life of poverty, that's all right. But what have you got against my horse?

Talking with God is as natural to Tevye as talking with his wife. He uses his own words, his own sentiments, his own feelings, his own humor.

What is your conversation with God like, or what could it be like? Possibly you would tell him about those who are sick who could use his healing touch. Maybe you'd ask him to bless your currently unemployed friend with honest work that pays a fair wage. Perhaps you would lament to him about the state of our nation, or the fears you are facing. Maybe you share with God the pain you are feeling from a recent breakup. He wants to hear our joys, pains, concerns—all of it.

Jesus taught us to call God, the Creator of the universe, Father. As one would go to an earthly father, so we are invited to approach our heavenly Father: "Cast all your worries upon him because he cares for you" (1 Peter 5:7). And know "the eyes of the Lord are on the righteous and his ears turned to their prayer" (1 Peter 3:12), with a reminder "we have this confidence in him, that if we ask anything according to his will, he hears us" (1 John 5:14). The Old Testament includes many times when Moses spoke face to face with God, at the burning bush, and up on the mountains, especially when he received the Ten Commandments. God spoke to Moses and he to God.

Other examples of a person speaking with God are found in the Book of Psalms. It is a collection of hymns and prayers to God, mostly from King David. He seeks God and his presence in his life. David begs God for his mercy on him and on the people of Israel. He seeks safety from his enemies and praises God for his blessings. If one were to take the psalms—and other Scripture passages—and divide them into categories of prayers, a list might include Adoration, Contrition, Thanksgiving, and Supplications: ACTS. This is an often-used mnemonic device to help people remember these prayer categories. (Others have used Wow, Oops, Thanks, and Please [WOTP], but I find ACTS easier to remember.) Let's examine each letter of ACTS separately to understand this acronym better.

A Is for Adoration

> Let everything that has breath
> give praise to the LORD!
>
> PSALM 150:6

Adore means "to give worship, honor, or praise as a deity or as divine," says Oxford Languages' dictionary. The *Catechism* states, "Adoration is the first attitude of man acknowledging that he is a creature before his Creator. It exalts the greatness of the Lord who made us" (*CCC* 2628). To adore God is to humble ourselves for we are creatures of the Creator of all. To be humble in God's presence is to adore him. Adoration involves acknowledging God in his beauty, his majesty, and his might. "Enter his gates with thanksgiving, / his courts with praise," implores Psalm 100:4. Praise and adoration bring us closer to the Lord's very presence, the throne room of our king. It also helps us to grow in faith and trust as we acknowledge his majesty, power, and might. "God needs no applause," says *Youcat*, a catechism for youths. "But we need to express spontaneously our delight in God and the rejoicing in our hearts. We praise God because he exists and because he is good. We thereby join even now in the eternal praise of the angels and saints in heaven." This is a taste of heaven on earth, joining in the never-ending adoration and praise of God.

It is important to note that adoration is not thanksgiving, which means being grateful for what God has done. Adoration is about acknowledging the essence of who God is.

Adoration can take many forms. It can be as simple as saying, "I love you Lord!" or, "Glory to God in the highest!" or, "Praise God!" It can also involve stating who he is: "You are the Prince of Peace, Emmanuel, God with us, Creator of all." Many hymns and songs sing God's praises. One I particularly like is by Rich Mullins:

Our God is an awesome God
He reigns from heaven above
With wisdom, power, and love.

C Is for Contrition

Have mercy on me, God, in accord with your merciful love.

Psalm 51:3

When we recognize our position as God's creation with humility, we are often confronted with our shortcomings. God, the all-powerful, all-loving, all-merciful, deserves more from us than we ever can give him. This void between what God deserves and what we give him is caused by our sinful nature. None of us is exempt from this truth. Humility is not about beating ourselves up for things we have or have not done. It is about truthfulness. We are nothing without God, our Creator and life giver. Without him we cannot do good, we are sinful, fallen from grace. It is by his providence that we can love God and one another. So, when we turn from God, we choose inferior substitutes like power and pleasure, fame and fortune, to name a few.

God wants us to have an ever-growing relationship with him. When we choose against God, deciding to go to a ballgame rather than Sunday Mass, we are choosing the lesser in place of the greater. God does not want our sins to keep us from him, but rather to acknowledge the truth, say we are sorry, ask his forgiveness, and move on. Once we have confessed and God has forgiven us, he removes our sin from us. Says the psalmist:

As far as the east is from the west,
so far has he removed our sins from us.

PSALM 103:12

We need to be empowered, to choose to believe the truth of the gospel that our sins have been washed away and we are free. When we elect to hold on to our guilt, it builds up and can lead to issues like depression, anxiety, and fear.

Catholics go to the priest for the sacrament of reconciliation (confession). We confess our sins and are reconciled with God and the Church, the body of Christ. When we sin, we harm the body. Since we cannot ask forgiveness of each person in the body of Christ, we seek it from the priest, a representative of the Church. And when we, members of that same body, grow in holiness and thus in our relationship with God, the whole body benefits. Our actions never affect only ourselves.

Regularly receiving the sacrament of reconciliation is one of the best things you can do to grow in relationship with God. But confession does not always have to come in sacramental form. At the beginning of Mass, we seek God's forgiveness for our sins and shortcomings. We pray, "I confess to almighty God and to you my brothers and sisters, that I have greatly sinned...." Most sins—the smaller, venial sins—can be forgiven by confessing them directly to God and saying we are sorry as in saying an act of contrition. Other, more grave sins—referred to as mortal sins because they can be deadly to our soul and involve serious matters—are to be forgiven in sacramental confession. There are many guidelines to help determine if our sins are grave or venial. These can be found in the *Catechism* or by speaking with your parish priest.

Many find a Daily Examen to be helpful. This is usually done in the evening, before bed, and walks a person back through the day to see where one may have met God or turned from him. There are many forms of Daily Examens (see Appendix A). They help us see the truth of ourselves more clearly, help us grow in humility, and come to contrition.

T IS FOR THANKSGIVING

What do you possess that you have not received?

1 CORINTHIANS 4:7

Thanksgiving is being grateful for God's gifts: healings, blessings, forgiveness, comfort, and love, for example. "Thank God the hurricane stayed out at sea. Thank God Jane's cancer is in remission. Thank God that presentation went so well!" God, directly and indirectly, pours forth abundant blessings on each of us every day. Our ability to breathe is a gift from him. To have eyes to see a sunrise, ears to hear beautiful music, the ability to feel a warm hug are all God's blessings. Everything we have has its origins in God. The Scriptures encourage us to always give God thanks (samples, Appendix B): "In all circumstances give thanks, for this is the will of God for you in Christ Jesus" (1 Thessalonians 5:18). Notice it says "in all circumstances." God encourages us to give thanks even in trials and pains. As a parent disciplines a child, so God disciplines us. Discipline may look like harm, but it may help us grow in charity, humility, or long suffering. These are all fruits of the Holy Spirit, and we should give thanks for the opportunities to grow these gifts.

We can express our thankfulness in ordinary words, songs, and dance. Musician Matt Redman's song "10,000 Reasons" speaks of the abundance of reasons to give thanks to God. In the Disney film *Happy Feet*, the penguins sing out their song of love, except for one little guy who can't seem to express his song of love with words, leading him to dance with abundant joy. We can all be creative in finding ways to express our thanksgiving.

Having an attitude of gratitude can go a long way in boosting our mental health, and many tout its benefits. Unfortunately, some forget to whom we should be thankful. I have been to many Thanksgiving feasts where everyone around the table gives thanks for something or someone, yet may fail to thank the Giver of all gifts. Thankfulness to each other is important, but thankfulness as prayer means being grateful to the Giver of all that is good, true, and beautiful.

It is important to give thanks for answered prayer. Remember the story in the Gospel of Luke where Jesus heals ten lepers but only one returns to give thanks (see Luke 17:11–19)? We can be so forgetful sometimes. Before a medical test, one might say, "Please, Lord, let these results be good." Then after we receive the outcome and are pleased, do we remember to thank God?

It is also important to be thankful for blessings with eternal ramifications: faith, salvation, redemption, our Lord coming to earth as a human, Jesus' suffering and death that provides forgiveness of sin. One can also express gratitude for God's blessing on a neighborhood, school, state, nation, and world. Thankfulness, like so many other things, grows with repeated practice. At first you may list more obvious and simple things, but as you continue, you will notice that your prayers of thankfulness can become more profound and genuine. It's like a muscle. The more you use it, the stronger it grows.

Giving thanks for the good things we have received can also have ramifications beyond our own relationship with God. Some people like to tell others of the good things God has done for them. Some might call this a praise report. Telling a friend that you asked God for help and he answered your prayer may help another to grow in faith, encouraging that person to approach God with his or her own need. God heals and blesses us because he loves us, but also so that we can give witness to his power that others may believe (see John 3:11 and 4:39).

In Mark's Gospel, as Jesus gets into a boat, a man who had been demon-possessed begs to go with him. Jesus does not let him but says, "Go home to your family and announce to them all that the Lord in his pity has done for you" (Mark 5:19). So the man goes away and begins to tell the people in the town how much Jesus had done for him. Everyone is amazed.

Let us all strive to have an attitude of gratitude to God, the Giver of all gifts, and share that knowledge with others that they too may believe the Good News of salvation.

S IS FOR SUPPLICATION

Have no anxiety at all, but in everything, by prayer and petition, with thanksgiving, make your requests known to God.

PHILIPPIANS 4:6

Supplication means to ask for things. We all know how to do this, but do we ask the One who can give what we seek? Supplication is an act of faith. If I need a loan, I won't go to a poor friend because I already know she doesn't have the means to help. She may desire to help me, but she is not able. Instead I may ask a friend who is wealthy. She would have the means to give what I request, but does she have the desire? When we approach God, we express our faith that God indeed can (and wants to) give us what we desire. He loves us more than anyone on earth can love us. He is also omnipotent and all-knowing, meaning he knows whether our desire is good for us or those for whom we pray. A fourteen-year-old might ask for a car, but loving parents would know a car is not an appropriate gift. You may ask God for a particular job, but God may know that, in the end, this wouldn't be the best job for you. When we ask God for anything, it is important to remember to ask according to his holy will. As the Our Father states, "Thy will be done." Make your request known and then surrender the outcome to God's loving plan. This requires trust, but is anyone more trustworthy than your Creator?

It is important when you pray for someone, or yourself, to be specific. You may pray for Grandma by saying, "God I pray for Grandma." But if you do pray in such general terms, how would you know when God answers your prayer? Think of who your grandmother is and her needs. Then your prayer may be, "God, please help my grandmother get good help in her home," or, "God, help Grandma with her finances." Then, when you see your prayers answered, you can rejoice, give thanks, and perhaps tell someone of your answered prayers.

There are two kinds of supplications. Let's call them petition and intercession. Petition is directed to your own needs. Intercession is to stand between another and God, to ask on someone's behalf. "He is always able to save those who approach God through him, since he lives forever to make intercession for them" (Hebrews 7:25). Our ability to approach God, the almighty and all-powerful, is only through Jesus Christ, the perfect intercessor. Our Lord said, "Whatever you ask in my name, I will do, so that the Father may be glorified in the Son" (John 14:13). Moses provides another great example of an intercessor:

Moses implored the LORD, his God, saying, "Why, O LORD, should your anger burn against your people, whom you brought out of the land of Egypt with great power and with a strong hand? Why should the Egyptians say, 'With evil intent he brought them out, that he might kill them in the mountains and wipe them off the face of the earth'? Turn from your burning wrath; change your mind about punishing your people. Remember your servants Abraham, Isaac, and Israel, and how you swore to them by your own self, saying, 'I will make your descendants as numerous as the stars in the sky; and all this land that I promised, I will give your descendants as their perpetual heritage.'" So the LORD changed his mind about the punishment he had threatened to inflict on his people.

EXODUS 32:11–14

If it weren't for Moses, the Israelites would have been exterminated. The saints, too, are wonderful intercessors. Saint Thérèse is the patron saint of missionaries; St. Joseph, of fathers and workers; St. Lucy, of eye disorders; and St. Gerard, of expectant mothers. As each of us has areas of concern and interest, so too do the saints. It is these interests that encourage their efforts in interceding for us. The saints themselves have little power. It is God alone who has the authority and ability to answer prayer. As we might ask a friend to pray for us, so we can request the prayers of the saints who are already in God's presence and find special favor with him.

There are so many people in the world with no one to pray for them: cancer sufferers, the grieving, the poor, the hungry, or the lonely. I have been taught to include them in my prayers by extending my request. I might pray for a relative battling cancer: "Oh God, I pray for Cathy, and all those who are struggling with cancer. Please ease their pain." Or, "God, please bless Paul—and all the unemployed—with a good job and a fair wage." And just like that, millions of people are prayed for. Isn't that amazing? The power we have with God to be a blessing to the world is so incredible and never-ending. It is important to remember that we do not have the power. God does. When we intercede, we ask God to use his power. Our desire to pray for another is an expression of love. It is that love that God responds to. Our participation in that love makes God's blessings, goodness, and healing go around.

Spiritual bouquets (see Simplecatholicliving.com) are wonderful ways to let others know you are praying for them. A spiritual bouquet is a list of prayers or sacrifices the giver is offering on behalf of the recipient. To be prayed for is wonderful. To know you are being prayed for is even better. It gives encouragement and love to the receiver. You can make a special card, use a preprinted one, or any piece of paper to list your offering. One example would be to offer a rosary, a novena, or a fast for that person's needs. The fast doesn't have to be extensive. I have fasted one spoon of sugar in my tea for a friend until she received work. These activities, in addition to being beneficial on their own, are expressions of love. The time you put into your bouquet is a precious witness of your love for him or her.

REFLECTION QUESTIONS

1. *Take some time to think of the things you have prayed for. See if they could be placed into these four simple categories: adoration, contrition, thanksgiving, or supplication. Would you add another category? If so, what would it be?*

2. *Open your Bible and read a few psalms. How do they fit into the categories of adoration, contrition, thanksgiving, and supplication (ACTS)?*

3. *Have you ever become speechless when given a gift from a loved one or friend? Yet, this is only an earthly gift. Have you ever been speechless before God for his abundant gifts to you? What gifts might make you speechless?*

4. *What are some benefits of conversational prayer? What might be some shortcomings?*

CHAPTER 4

Meditation and Contemplation

Finally, brothers, whatever is true, whatever is honorable, whatever is just, whatever is pure, whatever is lovely, whatever is gracious, if there is any excellence and if there is anything worthy of praise, think about these things.

PHILIPPIANS 4:8

Checking in on Sally, our friend from the introduction, we find she now has many ways she can intercede for her friend and the friend's daughter, including litanies, fasts, and novenas. Now Sally finds herself drawn to prayer, not just to help someone else but because she likes feeling close to God. Prayer gives her peace and strength to face the difficulties of her day. The prayers we have spoken about are good for this, but is there something more?

The prayers we have been examining up to this point would all be classified as vocal prayer. Whether we pray them aloud or quietly in our mind, they are still vocal. There are two other expressions of prayer: meditation and contemplation. In any genuine conversation, there is speaking and listening. Meditation and contemplation focus more on listening to God. We all know the experience of being talked to, in which the other person does not seek to know our thoughts, ideas, or reactions. That person never gets to know us. God wants us to speak with him, to share with him our hopes, dreams, and desires. But God also wants us to know him more fully. It is exactly this knowing that is the genuine goal of prayer. Many know of God intellectually, but to truly know him in our hearts is different. Many have received numerous teachings about God over the years, but still not know him. I can read a biography of a historical figure, but would I truly know her—or rather, do I know some things about her?

> [Jesus said,] Now this is eternal life, that they should know you, the only true God, and the one whom you sent, Jesus Christ.
>
> JOHN 17:3

Eternal life is all about getting to know God. The amazing truth of this is that we can begin this knowing here and now. When I read this passage from the Gospel of John quoting our Lord, it changed my life. I don't have to die and go to heaven to begin this knowing. God invites us to taste this knowing. That is the goal of our very lives now, today! What are we waiting for?

MEDITATION

It is this coming to know God that brings us to meditation and contemplation. Meditation is the work of the mind; contemplation is the work of the heart. To meditate on something is to ruminate, to chew on it, think it over, view it from various angles. One might meditate on an item from the news, trying to understand how a crisis affects people from different backgrounds. Christian meditation involves a focus on God, to reflect on or think about him. Meditation involves not just our mind but our imaginations, feelings, and will.

If I were to meditate on the birth of Jesus, I might reflect on what Mary was feeling: Was she scared, peaceful, or filled with joy? Did she feel God's presence with her? Was she confused, as this did not seem the right place for a king to be born? How could this be? How might I feel if this were me? By meditating on Scripture, we enter the scene. We can also reflect on what that passage may be saying to us today in our life and circumstance. Does our current situation make it difficult to understand God's purposes? Why don't things turn out as we planned? In this way, we can allow the Scripture to speak to us today, making it our own.

While the Bible is used most frequently in meditation, there is an abundance of other material we can use as well. We could use a divine truth or mystery like salvation or the Incarnation. We could meditate on the lives of the saints or even how God reveals his beauty and majesty in nature, remembering that we are seeking to connect with the Creator, not nature itself.

Many Catholic devotionals can help us meditate: *Prayers and Devotions from Pope John Paul II, Mary Day by Day, 365 Devotions for Catholics, Daily Moments with God*, and *Daily Reflections on Divine Mercy*. Many Christian-based ones are also good: *Grace for the Moment, Jesus Calling, Trusting God Day by Day*, and *365 Days of Prayer for Women*. One for couples is called *Night Light*. There are also devotionals for meditation available on Kindle, websites, and phone apps. Remember, not all books that offer meditations are Catholic or even Christian. Be sure to read the description. Ordering from Catholic sources such as Liguori Publications, Ave Maria Press, the Word Among Us, and others can give you confidence in your selection.

You may also look for the *nihil obstat* (nothing obstructs) and *imprimatur* (let it be printed). During the Council of Trent in 1563, the Church saw the need to have an indication to show the faithful that a particular book or pamphlet adhered to Catholic doctrine. Thus, people trying to grow in relationship with God would not be led astray with false or heretical teachings.

The nihil obstat and imprimatur are issued by the local bishop. But they do not mean that the bishop—or the Church—agree with the opinions or statements expressed in the product, but that the work does not oppose Church teachings. (This book was granted an imprimatur.) Today you will sometimes see a work was "printed with ecclesiastical permission." This statement also means the contents are free of doctrinal or moral error. These approvals are important in helping people find books and devotionals that are in line with magisterial teachings.

Some people like guided meditations, where you listen to someone who encourages you to use your imagination and follow along on a short journey to encounter God. These have become particularly popular through various apps. It is important to be discerning in using these guided meditations. While many can be fruitful in helping us connect with God, some can lead us into spiritualities that are non-Christian. Not everything, whether it mentions God or not, seeks to help you connect with our God whom we seek, Father, Son, and Holy Spirit. This is particularly true when the meditation refers to "spirit guides." Not all "spirits" are holy. Many disguise themselves as holy but, in truth, seek to degrade our relationship with God rather than build it up.

On a similar topic, please remember these points about Christian versus Eastern meditation practices. Many Christians unknowingly follow Eastern practices with the idea that all meditation is good and holy. But the goal of Eastern meditations, including Buddhist practices, have different outcomes in mind. They often encourage you to empty your mind and suggest you are in control of all things. Christian meditation is about opening your mind to God and acknowledging that he is in control of all things. Eastern meditation often seeks to relieve stress. This is a temporary relief, whereas Christian meditation is about encountering the one God, who can offer authentic peace and healing the world cannot give (see "7 Ways Christian Meditation Differs from Eastern Religions" on Beliefnet.com). It is important to nourish our souls with good food that leads us to God the Father, God the Son, and God the Holy Spirit.

CONTEMPLATION

Christian contemplation is like meditation in that the goal is to connect with God. Contemplation is more of a way of quiet and silence, a prayer of the heart. It is focused on God—wordless but not empty. An example would be when we gaze on a sleeping child and our hearts overflow with love so no words are needed. In a similar way, we connect with God.

When I first began to pray this way, I didn't know anything about it. I just found myself drawn to sit quietly with Jesus inside the church. I knew my Lord was present—Body, Blood, soul, and divinity—in the Blessed Sacrament. I wanted to connect with him, but I didn't feel the need to talk. When others asked why I was there, I would explain I was going for my "radiation" therapy. God's rays of love would come to me and touch the hurting, broken parts of me with his perfect healing and peace. Contemplation reminds me of a story St. John Vianney (1786–1859) told about an old farmer who would go to the church each day and sit in front of the tabernacle. When someone asked the farmer what he did there, he replied, "I look at him and he looks at me. We are happy together."

Prayer in the presence of the Blessed Sacrament is a great way to connect with God and experience his presence. Adoration chapels are more available for everyone to visit each day, to focus on the indwelling of God: Father, Son, and Holy Spirit. Adults often ask small children, "Where is Jesus?" The kids point to their heart and say, sometimes sheepishly, sometimes boldly: "Here." This is a great and awesome mystery and truth. God dwells within you and me, within all the baptized, as we see throughout the New Testament. While sin diminishes our ability to recognize God within, it does not remove God from us. God is always present, whether we realize it or not. Jesus said, "Whoever loves me will keep my word, and my Father will love him, and we will come to him and make our dwelling with him" (John 14:23). While this presence is not the same as the Blessed Sacrament being in the tabernacle inside a Catholic Church, God truly dwells within us. In this way we are like living tabernacles, bringing God to the supermarket, the ballfield, our workplace, the classroom, and to the whole world.

Contemplation, then, is "directing our attention to the presence of God dwelling in our heart," writes Fr. Martin Pable in *Prayer: A Practical Guide*. This loving awareness of God's indwelling, called contemplative prayer, is available twenty-four hours a day, seven days a week, wherever we are. Waiting in line at a supermarket, in traffic, anywhere and everywhere, we can turn our attention to God's presence.

Engaging in contemplative prayer opens our capacity to love by freeing our lives of anything that blocks or hinders it, according to Thomas H. Green in *Opening to God: A Guide to Prayer*. This freedom enables us to grow even more in our love of God and neighbor. "By being immersed in the presence and love of God we are transformed by his grace and more fully in tune with the will of God," Fr. Pable writes. In other words, we grow in holiness.

This growth in holiness through contemplative prayer often involves sitting quietly, striving to be aware of God's presence. This can seem like a waste of time, like nothing is happening, especially in the beginning. Our experience of prayer, our feelings and moods, are not good indicators of God at work within us. Our feelings and moods can be affected by our worries and fears, our health and that of our family—even our diet and exercise or lack thereof. Just because we don't feel God's presence is not an indication of his lack of presence. It is never a waste of time to spend time with God.

One time I was on a retreat with God, and I was so distracted and bored. I kept seeing signs around the grounds quoting the Book of Hosea, the prophet, that said, "Therefore, behold I will allure her, and will lead her into the wilderness: and I will speak to her heart" (Hosea 2:14). I thought: *OK. God, speak to me.* Then I realized Hosea said, "Speak to her heart," not her mind. God can speak straight to our hearts. If we choose to reach out to him, we will see beyond a doubt that he chose to reach for us first!

Saint Teresa of Calcutta experienced dryness—a lack of experiencing God's presence in prayer—for many years. This feeling did not hold her back from praying each day and growing in holiness. She trusted in him who loved her abundantly. When God's children trust him more than their own feelings, it is a sign of their love for God.

Saint Teresa of Ávila, a doctor of the Church noted for her insights into the journey of prayer, said in her autobiography that one of her biggest temptations was to give up on prayer because it was such a struggle. It is helpful to remember not to run after distractions but to let them float by. Otherwise, your prayer time can become one long battle against distractions.

While other types of prayer are considered active, contemplation is a passive prayer. It is the Holy Spirit praying within the person:

In the same way, the Spirit too comes to the aid of our weakness; for we do not know how to pray as we ought, but the Spirit itself intercedes with inexpressible groanings. And the one who searches hearts knows what is the intention of the Spirit, because it intercedes for the holy ones according to God's will.

Romans 8:26–27

While we may feel that all the effort during our prayer time is ours alone, God himself—through the Spirit—is speaking to the Father on our behalf. Sometimes prayer might feel like a waste of time, like nothing is happening but this is not true. God is always at work in us!

Another type or way to practice contemplative prayer is called centering prayer, which involves finding a peaceful place to sit and pray, then taking a few minutes to quiet any thoughts. Next, choose a word or phrase that links you to God and use this during your prayer time. Some use the name of Jesus. Others use "God saves," "Father," or a line from Scripture like, "Praise my soul the king of heaven," "The Lord is my strength," or "Peace be with you." From the earliest centuries of Christianity, some have used the Jesus Prayer: "Lord Jesus Christ, Son of the living God, be merciful to me a sinner." Then, once a phrase is chosen, the person praying slowly brings this word or phrase to mind a few times. Next, sit quietly with God. If your mind begins to wander, repeat the word(s) again to bring your attention back to God. This is not meant to be a mantra. Remember that you are not emptying your mind but being attentive to God's presence within. This can be done for a few minutes or longer. Most people I know who practice centering prayer start with five to ten minutes and then expand to fifteen minutes of prayer or more as the Lord leads.

I'd like to distinguish this kind of loving awareness from what many call "infused contemplation"—a supernatural gift from God—which usually occurs when we have put ourselves in quiet, contemplative prayer. Your attention and heart are caught up with God. You feel very in tune with your surroundings, without being distracted from God's presence. It can last a few moments or much longer. No matter the amount of time, you will know something special has happened. There is a sense of sweetness to it—not the kind you can taste in your mouth but a spiritual sweetness. As it is a supernatural gift, God gives it when and to whom he wants. We cannot produce this. We can, however, dispose ourselves to receive this gift by quieting ourselves and focusing on God. This gift of infused contemplation can come during any time of prayer: while reading Scripture, praying a rosary, after receiving holy Communion, or anytime we open our hearts to God. I have found it happens most often when I am praying contemplatively—the prayer of quiet. We should not go in search of this gift, but should remain open to receive it if God wills it. The more we seek to unite ourselves with God in prayer, the more likely we are to receive this intimate gift.

PRAYING WITH SCRIPTURE

Your word is a lamp for my feet,
a light for my path.

PSALM 119:105

In writing about meditation as an expression of prayer, I said that sacred Scripture, the Bible, is the best source of meditation. Over and over, particularly in the Book of Psalms, we are encouraged to meditate on the law of the Lord, day and night (see Psalm 1:2) and "on the glorious splendor of your majesty, / and on your wondrous works, I will meditate" (Psalm 145:5, *New Revised Standard Version, Catholic Edition*). "It is written: 'One does not live by bread alone, but by every word that comes forth from the mouth of God'" (Matthew 4:4).

Before we go any further, I will offer a word on translations: There are more than fifty different translations of sacred Scripture available, so it can feel quite daunting to choose one. I prefer the Catholic translations because I can be confident in the authenticity of the translators and the canon. The *New American Bible, Revised Edition* (*NABRE*) and the *New Revised Standard Version, Catholic Edition* (*NRSV-CE*) are the two more common ones recommended for Catholics. The *NABRE* is the easier of the two to read and is the one approved for use at Mass. The *NRSV-CE* is used more as a study edition. Both are excellent and succeed in allowing a person to know God and his word. In the end, as a friend once told me, the best translation is the one you will read!

This leaves the question of how to go about praying with Scripture. As with other forms of prayer, there are various ways to fit a variety of people with their differing faith journeys. Also, one way may fit you better at one time in your life than another. The first thing to do is to offer a prayer to the Author of the Scriptures—that is, the Holy Spirit. Catholics believe the Bible is inspired, meaning that what is written is what God wanted to be written. It was God and the human author working together. In this way, Scripture is unlike any other text we might read. Scripture is the very word of God. "In the beginning was the Word, and the Word was with God, and the Word was God," begins the Gospel of John (1:1). Jesus is the Word made flesh! Each encounter with Scripture is an encounter with God. If you see a Bible verse printed on a sign, that is an encounter with God. If you hear a song based on Scripture, that is an encounter with God. Before spending time in prayer with Scripture, it is suggested that we ask the Holy Spirit to come be with us and help us connect with God through his word.

The next step is deciding where to start. "In the beginning," you might assume. When it comes to Scripture, that may not always be the best place. One idea is to start with the daily

Bible readings for Mass. This works well for many people because you then are reading through the Bible in accordance with the liturgical calendar. During Advent, the readings are themed around the coming of Jesus. Around Lent, the readings are more about the forty days of prayer and fasting. Also, this creates continuity with the readings from Sunday Mass. Many aids are available, if this is where you would like to start praying with Scripture. *Breaking Open the Word* from Liguori Publications is a popular one.

The Gospels of Matthew, Mark, Luke, and John are other good places to start. Based on the life of Jesus, these books hold a preeminent place in all of Scripture. These are the readings we stand up for at Mass. Of all Scripture, these are the most familiar. Interestingly, many find parts of Scripture they know very well and parts they may have never read before. Being familiar with parts of the Bible does not ever get in the way of our ability to connect with God through Scripture. In fact, familiarity may facilitate a connection.

So now you are about ready to start. You have your Bible, prayed to the Holy Spirit, and chosen where to begin. There are two ways to read Scripture—for information or for inspiration. Many people have read the Bible simply for information—non-Christian historians for example. Some read it to satisfy curiosity. Atheists may read it to denounce Christian beliefs. Because time spent in prayer must include an opening of your heart to God, it's important to read the Bible for inspiration, to connect with God, and not just for information.

As you begin, let's say you choose to start with the Gospel of Matthew, the first book of the New Testament. Some people read from bold heading to bold heading. This is called a *peri-cope*. After you read a pericope, sit with it, maybe read it a few times. Meditate on it, chew on it, as we discussed in the previous chapter. What is it saying? Imagine how you might feel in the biblical scene. What might God be saying to you today through this scene? You might sit with it for a few minutes or longer, based on how God moves you.

Another way to pray with Scripture is to read until something catches your attention. This might be a paragraph or as much as a page or two. Often when something grabs your attention, it is good to sit with it. It may be the Holy Spirit speaking to you, saying there is something there for you to learn or a new way to connect with God. Again, you can stay with it as long as you feel moved to do so. Then you can continue reading from there or stop until the next day. The goal of praying with Scripture is to connect with God. There is no hurry.

LECTIO DIVINA

Lectio divina is an ancient prayer form dating back to around the year 220. It simply means "holy reading." It is a way of reading a holy text for spiritual nourishment that involves reflection and meditation. While *lectio divina* has only a few simple steps, there are many formats that enable it to be used in private and group settings.

The steps are reading (*lectio*), meditation (*meditatio*), prayer (*oratio*), and contemplation (*contemplatio*). Some add the additional step of action (*actio*). After a prayer to the Holy Spirit, you would read the passage the first time to glean information from the passage (*lectio*). Then pause and let the information soak in. In meditation (*meditatio*), you would read the passage a second time and then "walk around the passage." Who is present? How might each character perceive the situation? Are there different perspectives? How does the passage make you feel? Why are those characters in that scene? What might the author be trying to say through each person? After a brief pause, pray (*oratio*). In this step, reread the passage slowly and pause again.

What from this passage seems to speak to you? Is there a word or phrase that stands out? Speak with God about it. After a brief pause, reread the passage again. The next step is contemplation (*contemplatio*). Here you would rest in God's presence and with what was revealed to you during this Scripture. If you add an action (*actio*), you can include another reading of the passage and reflect on how the Scripture might change your behavior or future actions. Some readings that are good to begin with: the "Canticle of Mary" (Luke 1:46–55), the "Resurrection of Jesus" (Luke 24:1–12), the "Beatitudes" (Matthew 5:1–10), the "Man Born Blind" (John 9:1–12), the "Woman Caught in Adultery" (John 8:1–11), and the "Lord Is My Shepherd" (Psalm 23).

There are also many formats for praying *lectio divina* as a group. Sometimes one person does the readings four times. Other times different people read it each round. The first time it is read, get a sense of what the Scripture is saying. Then pause. Read it again slowly to allow it to speak to the group. Pause again. Does a word or phrase stand out to you? If so, share it with the group. Some groups share how it speaks to them. Others share the word or phrase. Read the passage again slowly, asking God what he would like to say to you through this passage. Share if you want. Read it again slowly. Now formulate a prayer to God based on what he was saying to you. Read it one last time, resting with God. Each group may do it differently, so be sure to get directions before beginning.

A practice many find helpful, especially when praying with Scripture, is to keep a spiritual journal. You might take note of what passages speak to you, what you sensed God might be saying to you, and any outcomes or takeaways you might have from that time of prayer. I find that when I look back at my journal, I see more clearly how God has been working. This is especially helpful when I feel discouraged in prayer. The journal can contain whatever you feel moved to include. I sometimes write letters to God when my prayer feels particularly stuck. As I write, I find the deeper reality of what was bothering me or holding me back. Then I can bring that to prayer. Some write poetry, track prayers requested and answered—anything that relates to our journey with God.

All prayer falls into one of these expressions or a combination of the three: vocal, meditative, or contemplative. For instance, the rosary is prayed with your voice, but we are called to meditate on the mysteries of the life of Jesus and may even find ourselves drawn into contemplation. Many find that starting their time of prayer vocally or meditatively sets the stage for contemplative prayer. It is all good, beautiful, and dynamic to connect with the living, true God: Father, Son, and Holy Spirit.

REFLECTION QUESTIONS

1. *Name the three expressions of prayer. How are they different?*

2. *What sources might someone use for meditation? Which might you feel more drawn to? Why?*

3. *How is Christian meditation different from Eastern meditation?*

4. *When you meet someone for the first or second time do you find that you both talk on and on with little or no silence? How about friends you have had for five, ten, or even twenty years? How do you feel about the silence? Are you more comfortable with it when you know the person better?*

5. *Contemplation is seeking to be attentive to God's indwelling presence. What might be some benefits of this type of prayer?*

6. *What is one thing to look for to know a book or pamphlet does not contain any doctrinal or moral error?*

7. *Follow the steps for* lectio divina *using Psalm 139:13–18. Describe the experience.*

FURTHER READING

Gallagher, Timothy M. *Meditation and Contemplation: An Ignatian Guide to Praying with Scripture.* New York: The Crossroad Publishing Company, 2008.

Giallanza, Joel. *I Consider the Labor Well Spent: A Mini-course on the Interior Castle.* Tucson: Edizioni Carmelitane, 2008.

Hall, Thelma. *Too Deep For Words: Rediscovering* Lectio Divina. New York: Paulist Press, 1988.

McBride, Denis. *Praying the Rosary: A Journey through Scripture and Art.* Liguori, Missouri: Liguori Publications, 2014.

Simsic, Wayne. *Seeking the Beloved: A Prayer Journey with John of the Cross.* Frederick, Maryland: The Word Among Us Press, 2012.

CHAPTER 5

Liturgical Prayer

Let us encourage one another to walk joyfully,
our hearts filled with wonder, towards our encounter
with the Holy Eucharist.

POPE BENEDICT XVI

The prayers we have examined thus far could all be categorized as private prayer. The goal of private prayer is the individual's intimacy with God. Alternatively, dictionaries say *liturgy* means "the work of the people" or a "service in the name of or on behalf of the people." In Christian tradition, liturgy means the participation of the people of God in the work of God. The people of God are all the baptized, the body of Christ. This description includes the Church militant (those living on earth and working toward the salvation of the world), and those who have gone before us, including the Church purgative (those in purgatory) and the Church triumphant (those in heaven). The work of God is the mending of our broken relationship with the Father, the result of the Fall of Adam and Eve. The mending is achieved through our Lord's redeeming sacrifice on the cross.

In liturgical prayer we enter and make present the paschal mystery: Jesus' suffering, death, and resurrection. It is not a reenactment or a redoing of the sacrifice. There was the one sacrifice of Jesus. We enter that moment as if we were present on Calvary on Good Friday. For this reason, the focus of liturgical prayer is not on the Church itself or its individual people but on God's desire for the salvation of the entire world, offered by Jesus and the people of God. It is the official prayer of the Church, with a prescribed ritual format that includes not only words but gestures, symbols, and postures. While there is room for some adjustments for local customs, there is very little that is changed from place to place. We are then united in the one prayer.

This distinction between liturgical and private prayer does not rely on the number of people involved. A thousand people praying a rosary is not liturgical. In the same vein, a few people gathering for Mass is not private prayer. Private prayer is intended to unite the individual with God through Christ, even when this prayer is being done for another. The aim is intimacy with God. Liturgical prayer, it could be said, forms us into the body of Christ. We become one with each other and with Christ. A prayer life is at its best when it contains both liturgical and private prayer. Private prayer enriches liturgical prayer and liturgical prayer nourishes private prayer.

"The liturgy is the summit toward which the activity of the Church is directed; it is also the font from which all her power flows," says the Second Vatican Council's Constitution on the Sacred Liturgy (*Sacrosanctum Concilium*). All the graces we receive and all the good we do find their sources in liturgical prayer. "Through the liturgy Christ, our redeemer and high priest, continues the work of our redemption in, with, and through his Church" (*CCC* 1069).

Only a few prayers are considered liturgical prayer. The most common are the sacraments, especially the Mass; the Divine Office, also called the Liturgy of the Hours; and the liturgical calendar. The Mass is considered the perfect prayer, Jesus' sacrificial offering of himself that we enter and share in. The Liturgy of the Hours is an extension of the Mass and so also enters into the saving work of Christ on the cross. The liturgical calendar includes the seasons: Advent, Christmas, Lent, Easter, and Ordinary Time. It also includes the solemnities, feast days, and memorials celebrated throughout the year. Each time we celebrate these liturgical events, we are connected with the Mass, and therefore it is liturgical prayer. The Advent wreath, Lenten fasts, feast days for the saints, and Marian holy days are all examples of prayer with the liturgical calendar.

THE MASS

All prayer is a vessel to grow in union with God. The Mass, where we gather as a community to celebrate the Eucharist, is the vessel *par excellence.* It is a profound encounter with the Holy Trinity: God the Father, God the Son, and God the Holy Spirit. In it we are enriched and strengthened to live our daily lives. For many, the Mass gives a sense of peace and belonging in a way the world cannot offer. We find purpose and mission for our day-to-day lives and a sense of a greater purpose for our existence. We can find solace and consolation in troubling times, rejoicing and beauty in better times. Whether we feel broken or on top of the world, the Mass has much to offer us.

We may go to Mass to receive food for our journey on earth. This is wonderful itself. But as liturgical prayer, it is also the work of the people, the source and summit of our faith. It is through the saving action of Christ on the cross, which we enter into and make present, that our faith in salvation is rooted. It is also all we ultimately hope for, to spend eternity in heaven with God. We can see salvation in terms of our own personal salvation, but it is also about the salvation of the world. This is God's greatest desire and the Church's stated mission. "This is good and pleasing to God our savior, who wills everyone to be saved and to come to knowledge of the truth" (1 Timothy 2:3–4). In St. John Paul II's encyclical *Redemptoris Missio,* he states that all the baptized are called to participate in this great mission of bringing Christ to all the world, that they may know him and be redeemed. While you may not feel you get much out of Mass on Sunday, it is the mission of the Church to which we belong to pray for the world, our families, and ourselves.

The Liturgy of the Word and the Liturgy of the Eucharist comprise the structure of the Mass at its most basic. In the Liturgy of the Word, which contains the Scripture readings for the day, the Church grows in wisdom by presenting a model to live our life in God, with his mind and his purposes. In the Liturgy of the Eucharist, the eucharistic prayers, and distribution of holy Communion, the Church and we personally grow in holiness and are given effective power to live out God's will and purposes, says Emily Strand, MA, in *Mass 101*. This call of God to grow in holiness never ends. The closer we get to God, the more fervently he calls us to come even closer and the more graces God bestows on us to respond.

In the Mass, we encounter Christ personally in many ways. Vatican II's *Sacrosanctum Concilium* describes four ways Christ is present within the Mass. First, he is present in the priest, *in persona Christi*, offering sacrifice to the Father. Next, he is present in the assembly gathered. Jesus Christ says in the Gospel, "Where two or three are gathered together in my name, there am I in the midst of them" (Matthew 18:20). The Holy Spirit dwells in the heart of all the baptized, so when the baptized gather, God is present. Third, Christ is present in his word proclaimed. The very beginning of the Gospel of John says, "In the beginning was the Word, and the Word was with God, and the Word was God" (John 1:1). Later it says, "The Word became flesh and made his dwelling among us" (John 1:14). When the readings are proclaimed, Jesus is made manifest in those words. Fourth, our Lord is most profoundly present in the Eucharist, in his Body and Blood. While we encounter Christ in his word, in the assembly, and in the priest, we can only encounter his Real Presence, in the fullest sense, in the Eucharist.

> This presence is called "real," ...which is not intended to exclude the other types of presence as if they could not be "real" too, but because it is presence in the fullest sense: that is to say, it is a substantial presence by which Christ, God and man, makes himself wholly and entirely present (*CCC* 1374).

In St. John Paul II's encyclical on the Eucharist in Its Relationship to the Church (*Ecclesia de Eucharistia*), he writes:

> In a variety of ways she (the Church) joyfully experiences the constant fulfillment of the promise: 'Lo, I am with you always, to the close of the age' (Matthew 28:20), but in the Holy Eucharist, through the changing of bread and wine into the body and blood of the Lord, she rejoices in this presence with unique intensity.

More than the Church and its people are grateful to God for the Eucharist, asserts Pope Francis in "On Care for Our Common Home" (*Laudato Si'*, 236):

> In the Eucharist all that has been created finds its greatest exaltation....Joined to the incarnate Son, present in the Eucharist, the whole cosmos gives thanks to God.... The Eucharist joins heaven and earth; it embraces and penetrates all creation." In the bread of the Eucharist, the world which came forth from God's hands returns to him in blessed and undivided adoration.

Christ is present in the Eucharist in a real and substantial way. This is not a symbolic presence. In John 6:53, "Jesus says [to his disciples], 'Amen, amen, I say to you, unless you eat the flesh of the Son of Man and drink his blood, you do not have life within you.'" Believing this to be an impossible teaching, many people began to walk away. At this point Jesus did not say, "Wait, don't go away! I only meant this symbolically!" He watched them leave and continued with his teaching. The truth that simple bread and wine are transubstantiated into Christ's Body, Blood, soul, and divinity is hard to imagine. The depths of this sacred mystery are too much for us to fully grasp. Yet, we can always grow in our understanding of it. Over the centuries God has performed many miracles to help us believe this truth.

A few years ago, I had the wonderful opportunity to travel to Medjugorje, a town in Bosnia and Herzegovina, where many believe the Blessed Mother has been appearing to four people at varying times over the past four decades. While I was there, pilgrims were milling about, going up the mountain to where the apparitions first started, seeing the weeping crucifix, or even looking for a miracle in the sun. All of this was very uplifting for me, but on this day I was simply praying the rosary in a meditation garden. When I came to the Luminous Mystery of the institution of the Eucharist, I received an insight. We, humanity in general, look for signs and miracles to boost our faith, and they often do this. But somehow we tend to miss the greatest miracle of all time—transubstantiation. Simple bread and wine is turned into the very Body, Blood, soul, and divinity of Jesus Christ, the Son of God. We cannot see this with our physical eyes because the natural elements all remain the same: sight, smell, feel, and taste. This miracle takes the eyes of faith and a deep trust in the truths of our faith. We need to look beyond our physical senses. While I did physically see an unofficial miracle or two while I was there, the greatest miracle

I experienced was to grow in my understating and appreciation for the greatest miracle of all, transubstantiation.

At times, though, it may feel like nothing much is going on and we are not getting anything out of the Mass. I smile to myself when I think like this because it reminds me to realize that I'm like a sick person in the hospital with an intravenous line in my arm. I don't often notice it's there, but it's providing me much-needed hydration, nutrition, and medication. My father would often complain that the doctors would keep him in the hospital when "they weren't doing anything," but they were doing much more than he realized. They were monitoring his blood pressure, temperature, heart rhythm, providing medications, and were ready to respond on a moment's notice if he went into cardiac arrest again. Likewise, we may not feel like anything is happening when we go to Mass, yet we are being fed vital nutrition for the depths of our very selves.

While attending Mass on Sundays and holy days of obligation are important, mere attendance is not what we are called to do. As with all prayer, we must open our hearts to God so we may be inspired and draw closer to God. "Mother Church earnestly desires that all the faithful should be led to that fully conscious and active participation in liturgical celebrations which is demanded by the very nature of the liturgy. Such participation by the Christian people as 'a chosen race, a royal priesthood, a holy nation, a redeemed people' (1 Peter 2:9; see 2:4–5), is their right and duty by reason of their baptism" (*SC* 14).

How do we achieve full, active, and conscious participation? One way is to prepare for Mass—not just by getting dressed and driving there but by reviewing and praying with the readings beforehand. In this way, when we hear them proclaimed at Mass, we are not hearing them for information but inspiration. Another way involves engaging with the postures and gestures, being aware of what we are doing and why. Why do we stand for one reading and not others? Why do we make the sign of the cross on our forehead, lips, and heart before the reading? Why do we bow during part of the Creed? These things have meaning and help us be more conscious of the activities that bring beauty to the Mass. Participating in the responses and the singing also add to this full participation. The more we participate, the more grace we receive, and the more likely we are to experience contact with God. Being open to the grace offered during Mass is important. Grace is a gift. If we put the gift aside unopened, we don't get to use what the gift has to offer. If we receive the gift and unwrap it, like opening our hearts to receive grace, we get to enjoy the fullness of that gift.

A lack of understanding of the actions and purpose of the Mass can make it difficult to be fully present to the gift of the Mass. Without an understanding that reaches beyond our childhood days, how can we attempt to grow deeper into this unending mystery? To help, there have been many wonderful books written on the Mass. There is so much beauty and truth within the Mass that I can only scratch the surface here. I encourage you to do more reading. Your experience of Mass will never be the same. The books listed in the "Further Reading" section at the end of this chapter are a good place to start.

SACRAMENTS AS PRAYER

All the sacraments of the Church are forms of prayer. The Mass, the celebration of the Eucharist, is the sacrament from which all other sacraments flow. It is through the life, death, and resurrection of Christ that the sacraments flow. As with the Mass, there are many books written on the sacraments, but I will briefly touch on a few important points. There are seven sacraments: baptism, Eucharist, confirmation, reconciliation, anointing of the sick, marriage, and holy orders. Three are only available once per lifetime: baptism, confirmation, and holy orders. Marriage is meant to be celebrated only once, but in the event of the death of a spouse, it may be received again. Eucharist, reconciliation, and the anointing of the sick are available to be received frequently.

The old *Baltimore Catechism* states that a sacrament is "an outward sign, instituted by Christ to give grace." The "outward sign" refers to the water, the holy oil, the laying on of hands, the physical actions we can see. Saint Augustine wrote that sacraments are "visible signs of invisible grace." "Instituted by Christ" from the *Baltimore Catechism* means that all of the sacraments find their source in the life of Christ as written in sacred Scripture.

The purpose of the sacraments is to give grace. We often hear the word *grace*, but what is it? "Grace is first and foremost the gifts of the Spirit who justifies and sanctifies us" (*CCC* 2003). To sanctify us is to make us holy, more closely united with God. If the purpose of prayer is to unite us with God, then all the sacraments are forms of prayer.

Two sacraments I will examine more closely here are the sacraments of healing: reconciliation and the anointing of the sick. Reconciliation (confession) is available in nearly all Catholic churches each week. Every Saturday, Catholics used to line up for confession before Mass on Sunday. Nowadays, the lines may be rare. (One church I knew of in New York still had long lines every Saturday. I attributed this to the fact that they had perpetual eucharistic adoration in the parish, which can lead to personal growth in humility and holiness.) Priests also strive to make themselves available throughout the week for those who cannot attend on Saturday. In my experience, other than the Eucharist, reconciliation is the most beneficial thing I do that helps me on my journey with God.

Saint Teresa of Ávila speaks of how part of the journey to union with God is to know yourself. When we see ourselves as we truly are, in humility, we can see more clearly our need and dependence on God. Without God, I can do no good thing. I lived for many years with God on the periphery of my life. During that time, my life was filled with all sorts of sins: hurting many people by my words and actions, ignoring God and others. God provided opportunities for me to turn back to him, and I finally took advantage of them. When I turned back, I started to grow closer to God. I found his love and grace transforming me to be more loving, compassionate, and merciful. This sacrament is the one that leads us to be more honest about who we are—both good and bad—and to see both where God is at work inside our life and where we are keeping him outside.

As a teacher, one common complaint I've heard is why we have to go to a priest for confession. Can't God hear us wherever we pray? Indeed, God hears us wherever we are. The priest is a physical sign of our Church community. When we sin, we not only hurt our relationship with God but also that of the whole body of Christ to which we belong. It might be helpful to invoke sports metaphors. In baseball, if the pitcher is not at his best, the entire team usually suffers. If the running back in football keeps fumbling the ball, the other members of the team suffer. So, when I sin, I hinder the workings of the body of Christ. Thankfully the same can be said about growing in holiness. When my holiness grows, I add to the strength of the whole "team." In this sense, being Catholic is not a private matter. There is never a time when my personal sin is only about me. Many say, "Well, I'm not hurting anyone else with this sin." This is not the case.

Going to confession to a priest at the church is also a physical action we take to show our sorrow and remorse. We are physical beings. Thus, physical actions help us express our inner sentiments. If we've hurt a friend, the action of writing the person a note or going to speak with her or him is a sign of inner sorrow and remorse. Also, as a sacrament, confession enables us to receive grace to do better. Yes, we may confess the same sin again and again, but generally it undergoes subtle improvement each time, leading to a break in the cycle of that sin. The priest, directed by the Holy Spirit, can also give us advice or recommendations to break free from patterns that may lead us to sin.

In reconciliation I also find it helpful, though not always so easy, to go to just one priest. In this way, the priest and I develop a better understanding of where I might be committing habitual sin. In the confessional, the priest is more than a representative of the Church. He is acting *in persona Christi*, that is, "in the person of Christ." This sacred power has been passed down by Christ himself to his apostles and their successors: "In imparting to his apostles his own power to forgive sins, the Lord also gives them the authority to reconcile sinners with the Church" (*CCC* 1444). If reconciliation is a healing sacrament, then the aim is to fix what is broken in us. When we come face to face with what is broken, we can bring it to our Father in heaven to receive his healing and love. His healing grace transforms us. I personally feel lighter and more peaceful after having this life-giving contact with God through the person of the priest.

In the anointing of the sick, Catholics come forth in search of God's healing touch, comfort in their pain and suffering, and strength to endure. "He has come to heal the whole man, soul and body; he is the physician the sick have need of" (*CCC* 1503). The healing can be for matters of physical, mental, emotional, or even spiritual needs. This sacrament is administered by a priest and can be requested in times of serious suffering. It takes only a few minutes, yet the sacrament brings the presence and grace of God for healing of mind, body, and spirit.

Let's say Sally, our friend, was recently diagnosed with cancer. She's scared of what the future might hold and wishes it would just go away. She goes to her doctors, as she should, to receive the help they can offer. She may tell her family and friends, seeking their prayers and support. She may also turn to God in her private prayer or at Mass and ask God to help her and heal her. In the anointing of the sick she'd be turning to the ultimate healer and, given that it is a sacramental form of prayer, she would receive sacramental grace that is unavailable through ordinary means. The grace may be manifested through a sense of peace about her future, maybe through wisdom in terms of which doctors she turns to, perhaps strength to endure the suffering, or maybe even full and complete healing. God is the best giver of gifts, since only he knows what we truly need in our lives. As with any prayer, we may walk away not feeling any differently than before. This is not an indication of what has or has not happened. God's word can be trusted. When we seek him with a sincere heart, he will hear and answer us with the best he has to offer.

In my parents' day, the anointing of the sick was considered the sacrament of the dying and called "last rites." People nearing death would get fearful and ask that the priest not be called because when he gave you last rites your death was imminent. Thankfully, today we have a fuller understanding of the sacrament, not just as grace for crossing from this life to the next but as Christ's desire to heal us all along our journey in life.

In the sacraments we receive special grace called sacramental grace. There are seven sacraments, but by extension, grace can be received through prayers and devotions connected with those sacraments—the Mass in particular. I'm speaking of eucharistic adoration and benediction. In eucharistic adoration, the consecrated host is taken from the tabernacle and placed in a monstrance. The Blessed Sacrament is the Body, Blood, soul, and divinity of Christ. As discussed earlier, he is truly and substantially present in the consecrated host. The monstrance is then placed on the altar. The faithful then gaze on their loving and merciful Lord in silence, in song, or in prayers in his honor.

I have seen many videos of dignitaries and celebrities who go on bended knee before the queen of England. This is a sign of honor and respect. Here, in the consecrated host, we have the almighty God—Father, Son, and Holy Spirit—present before us. Some say, "I can't wait to get to heaven and see our Lord face to face." Well, he is right here. While our physical senses see only a plain host, it does not change the reality of who is present.

Many parishes offer Holy Hours throughout the year so the faithful can come to venerate and adore Christ in the Blessed Sacrament. There are many powerful graces available to those who come to a Holy Hour. An unattributed quotation reads, "Through our Holy Hours of prayer, Our Holy Father declares that we are contributing to 'the radical transformation of the world,' the 'establishing of everlasting peace,' and the coming of Christ's Kingdom on Earth."

Depending on the parish, the Holy Hour may include hymns, readings, a homily, a rosary, or other devotions. If a priest is present, benediction (meaning "blessing") is offered. During benediction, the priest or deacon carefully picks up the monstrance and, making the sign of the cross with it, blesses the people gathered. If you, like many, struggle to believe in Christ's Real Presence in the Eucharist, come to a Holy Hour and let him help your unbelief.

Some parishes have perpetual adoration. This is where our Redeemer is exposed in the Blessed Sacrament all the time. Many people commit to spending a particular hour with our

Lord in adoration every week. Together these hours add up to twenty-four hours a day, seven days a week. During perpetual adoration, anyone—parishioners, Catholics, Christians, even nonbelievers—are welcome to come in and spend time with the eucharistic Lord.

Earlier I mentioned going for my "radiation therapy" before the Lord. This can be done with Christ enclosed in the tabernacle or exposed in the monstrance. Our Lord is always present in the Eucharist in every Catholic church. He remains waiting for us to spend time with him in worship or simply in his presence. St. Thérèse of Lisieux wrote in a letter to her sister, Celine, "Oh, my darling, think, then, that Jesus is there in the tabernacle expressly for you, for you alone. He is burning with the desire to enter your heart." The Lord is waiting for you, waiting for me!

All prayer before the Blessed Sacrament is beneficial to us, our families, and the world. Saint John Paul II is quoted in the *Catechism*, saying, "The Church and the world have a great need for Eucharistic worship. Jesus awaits us in this sacrament of love. Let us not refuse the time to go to meet him in adoration, in contemplation full of faith, and open to making amends for the serious offenses and crimes of the world. Let our adoration never cease" (*CCC* 1380).

OTHER LITURGICAL PRAYERS

There are two more types of liturgical prayer: the liturgical calendar and the Liturgy of the Hours, sometimes called the Divine Office. Both flow from the celebration of the Eucharist. The liturgical calendar is the superimposing of the major events in the life of Christ throughout a calendar year. We have the birth of Christ, his years of ministry, his passion, death, resurrection, and ascension. We also have times of preparation for these great events, such as Advent and Lent. As part of these various celebrations, we see the priestly vestments and altar cloths change—particularly the colors—throughout the year.

The prayers and readings at Mass change with the seasons. For example, during Advent there are readings from the Old Testament telling of the coming of the Messiah. During Lent the readings focus on fasting and time in the desert. The Church year also includes celebrations in honor of Mary and other saints of the Church. In the season of Ordinary Time, we hear readings on the ministry and life of Jesus and how the early disciples lived out the gospel message. The season is termed "Ordinary" because its weeks are numbered. The Latin *ordinalis* refers to numbers in a series and comes from *ordo*, from which we derive the English word *order*. We enter into the liturgical calendar by participating in these experiences during the Church year: Advent wreaths, Lenten fasts and missions, Christmas and Easter traditions, Marian celebrations, and similar events.

As we enter a new liturgical year, we are also called to enter into the Liturgy of the Hours or Divine Office. The Liturgy of the Hours is a universal, public prayer of the Church that has been prayed in various forms since ancient times. It reaches from the celebration of the Mass to all hours of the day. Through this we sanctify, make holy, the entire day. Saint Paul urges us in 1 Thessalonians 5:17 to "pray without ceasing." While individuals may not be praying every minute of every hour of each day, the universal Church is offering these prayers on our behalf throughout the day. Given the various time zones and schedules, it is easy to imagine that at every minute someone in the Church is always praying the Liturgy of the Hours. Through it the "biblical readings lead the person who prays it ever deeper into the mystery of the life of Jesus Christ," says *Youcat*, the youth catechism. So, while praying it sanctifies the day, it also sanctifies those who pray it.

While some—such as priests, deacons, and religious—are bound by Church law to pray the Liturgy of the Hours, the lay faithful are also strongly encouraged to participate. Ideally, it is to be prayed communally, but it also may be prayed individually. Even if prayed individually, since it is liturgical prayer, the person is joined with others also praying it.

There are seven "hours" of the day: Office of Readings, Morning, Midmorning, Midday, Midafternoon, Evening, and Night Prayer. While some pray all the hours, some pray only the major hours of Morning Prayer, Evening Prayer, and Night Prayer. These hours are on a four-week cycle called a Psalter. Each hour consists of hymns, psalms, biblical readings, and intercessions. When taken together, it is a hymn of praise offered to the Father through all the ages.

Most prayer is private prayer, but liturgical prayer encompasses a large part of what we Catholics do. In liturgical prayer we find that the Blessed Mother Mary and the other saints of the Church are active in our prayer life. The next chapter will look at the saints of the Church and how they assist us on our journey of holiness.

REFLECTION QUESTIONS

1. *How are liturgical prayer and private prayer similar? How are they different?*

2. *What body postures are used during the Mass and at what times? What might a posture be saying about what is happening at that moment?*

3. *Without our full, active, and conscious participation, attending Mass can easily become mere actions and not a prayer. Most people go to Mass to encounter God. Some leave disappointed. What we take from the experience is linked in part to what we bring to it. What might you be able to change for your participation to become full, active, and conscious?*

4. *What are four ways God is present in the Mass? Which ones are you most familiar with? Is one a newer concept to you?*

5. *There are seven sacraments. What is the physical sign of each one? Which sacraments have you received? What do they mean to you?*

6. *What is the purpose of praying the Liturgy of the Hours individually and for the world?*

FURTHER READING

Catalogue of the Vatican International Exhibit. *The Eucharistic Miracles of the World*. Bardstown, Kentucky: Eternal Life, 2009.

Hahn, Scott. *The Lamb's Supper: The Mass as Heaven on Earth*. New York: Doubleday, 1999.

Randolph, Francis. *Know Him in the Breaking of the Bread: A Guide to the Mass*. San Francisco: Ignatius Press, 1998.

Saint John Paul II. Encyclical on the Eucharist in Its Relationship to the Church Encyclical (*Ecclesia de Eucharistia*). April 17, 2003.

Strand, Emily. *Mass 101: Liturgy and Life*. Liguori, Missouri: Liguori Publications, 2013.

Van Slyke, Daniel. *Liturgy 101: Sacraments and Sacramentals*. Liguori, Missouri: Liguori Publications, 2010.

CHAPTER 6

Praying with Mary and the Saints

In trial or difficulty I have recourse to Mother Mary,
whose glance alone is enough to dissipate every fear.

St. Thérèse of Lisieux

Mary, the Mother of Jesus and our Mother, is always there to guide us closer to Jesus. She is his mother and thus knows what pleases him the best. She is in no way part of the Holy Trinity. Believing that would be idolatry. She should never be worshiped or put above God; that is not her desire. She wants people to worship God—Father, Son, and Holy Spirit—as they deserve. She desires to assist all her children to draw as close as possible to her divine Son.

We believe, as St. Paul VI wrote in Credo of the People of God (*Solemni Hac Liturgi*), that the Blessed Mother of God, the New Eve, Mother of the Church, continues in heaven her maternal role with regard to Christ's members, cooperating with the birth and growth of divine life in the souls of the redeemed.

Praying with Mary

If you examine the many Church teachings on Mary through the centuries, you will find an abundance of titles for Mary: Our Lady, Mother of God, Queen of Angels, Star of the Sea, Mother of Mercy, Cause of our Joy, to name a few. You may already be familiar with some of them. Many titles for Mary, such as Mother of Jesus and the New Eve, are taken directly from sacred Scripture. Others are from Church doctrines, such as the Immaculate Conception and Virgin of Virgins. Each of these titles contain within them volumes of teachings on who Mary is and why the Church holds her in highest esteem. I cannot even touch on each of these in a short book, let alone do them justice. Instead, I will focus on one I have found particularly advantageous in my journey: Mary, the Mother of God.

This title holds great depth and beauty and has nourished my prayer with Mary. The Mother of God title was given to Mary to identify the truth of Jesus' full humanity and full divinity at the time of his birth. Many titles and dogmas arise to counter heresies, or false teachings. Some early Christians taught that Jesus was born fully human but did not become divine until later in his life. By declaring Mary as the Mother of God, the Church confirmed what it believed from the beginning—that Jesus was fully human and fully divine, thus making Mary the Mother of Jesus' humanity and divinity. This does not mean that Mary was the source of Jesus' divinity, but that the child who came forth from her womb was the Son of God.

Saint John Paul II, in his encyclical on the Blessed Virgin Mary in the Life of the Pilgrim Church (*Redemptoris Mater*), refers to the Council of Ephesus in 415 and states "the truth of the divine motherhood of Mary was solemnly confirmed as a truth of the Church's faith. Mary is the Mother of God, *Theotokos* in Greek, since by the power of the Holy Spirit she conceived in her virginal womb and brought into the world Jesus Christ, the Son of God, who is of one being with the Father."

Mary was and is special, even unique. She was not one of many God chose for this most important of tasks. She was not a mere vessel, but the one called to love and nurture the Son of God on earth. Mary was chosen by the Father for the Son, in union with the Holy Spirit. God chose her to be the first to believe the Good News, the first disciple of Jesus.

This incredible woman, so pure and lovely that all generations will call her blessed, was given to us at the foot of the cross to be our Mother, to help us not just on our journey on earth but also our journey into eternity. From the cross, Jesus said to her, "Woman, behold your son." And looking at the beloved disciple, he said, "Behold your mother" (John 19:25–26). In doing so, Jesus gave his own Mother to me and to you to help us on our journeys.

She is a powerful intercessor and perfect model of faith, humility, and discipleship. The saints testify to Mary as model and intercessor. "The greatest saints, those richest in grace and virtue, will be the most assiduous in praying to the most Blessed Virgin, looking up to her as the perfect model to imitate and as a powerful helper to assist them," St. Louis de Montfort said. Saint Padre Pio said, "May the mother of Jesus and our mother, always smile on your spirit, obtaining for it, from her most holy son, every heavenly blessing." Pope Benedict XVI wrote, "Let us entrust to her intercession the daily prayer for peace."

The greatest desire in the heart of Mother Mary is to bring us to her Son, Jesus. Saint Alphonsus Liguori wrote, "God, who loves Mary immensely," cannot "fail to hear her when she prays for sinners who recommend themselves to her." We are in good hands when we turn to Mary in our needs and desires. There is nothing she wants more than to assist us to love and be loved by her Son. All the Marian apparitions down through the centuries can be summed up by "pray and stay close to Jesus." And, staying close to Mary can help us remain close to Jesus.

Saint Thérèse of Lisieux was devoted to Mother Mary. She focused much on the ordinariness of Mary that could be imitated by everyone. This ordinariness makes Mary a great prayer partner. Sacred Scripture talks about us encouraging one another as we have been encouraged in Christ (see 2 Corinthians 1:3–7). It is in our struggles and pains that we gain almost a right to sit with one another sharing the same struggle. I remember many years ago when my first husband passed away suddenly, many came to comfort me saying, "I know how you feel." The reality is they didn't know what to say to a twenty-four-year-old widow. I didn't experience a true sense of comfort until someone came forth who was also a young widow and said, "I know."

Mary, because of her struggles and joys of ordinary life, can meet us in our pains and joys and sincerely say to us, "I know." When the angel asked her to be the mother of the long-awaited Messiah, she said yes to God's plan—despite not understanding how this could happen, despite the rejection and ridicule she might face. Many of us have faced times when God seems to be asking more than we can handle, but we choose to trust God and submit to God's will. Mary knows. Mary, faced with the hopeless situation of finding a place for the king of the universe to be born and settling for a stable, understands our struggles. We also fight when faced with the idea that the future for our child or loved one may not be as bright or sunny as envisioned. Mary struggled, knowing that many would oppose Jesus, as foretold by Simeon during the presentation of Jesus in the Temple. She understands how tired the young mom is rocking her sick child at 2 AM. She knows the sorrow of losing a parent, a spouse, and even her Son. She experiences the ordinary things in life, but by grace and her openness to God in her life, she allows them to be vessels for faith and love. I love the ordinariness of Mary, the Mother of God!

THE ROSARY

One means the Church encourages that I use to grow closer to God and the Blessed Mother is the rosary. Returning to St. John Paul II's apostolic letter *Rosarium Virginis Mariae*, "The Rosary of the Virgin Mary…is a prayer loved by countless saints and encouraged by the Magisterium. Simple yet profound, it still remains…a prayer of great significance" (*RVM* 1). Saint John Paul II frankly admitted, "The Rosary is my favorite prayer. A marvelous prayer. Marvelous in its simplicity and in its depth." He goes on to say that "Against the background of the words *Ave Maria* the principal events of the life of Jesus Christ pass before the eyes of the soul" (*RVM* 2).

Six fundamental prayers are in the rosary. The Sign of the Cross, the Apostles' Creed, the Our Father, the Hail Mary, the Glory Be, and the Hail Holy Queen. After the introductory prayers, the Hail Marys are recited in decades—that is, in groups of ten. Each decade is paired with a particular mystery in the life of Jesus and Mary upon which the person praying can focus or meditate. The five decades prayed together are grouped into various mysteries: the Joyful Mysteries focus on the annunciation (the message of the angel to Mary), the visitation (when Mary visits cousin Elizabeth), the birth of Jesus, the presentation of Jesus in the Temple, and the finding of Jesus in the Temple. The Luminous Mysteries focus on the ministry of Jesus: his baptism in the Jordan, the miracle at Cana, the proclamation of the kingdom, the transfiguration, and the institution of the Eucharist at the Last Supper. The Sorrowful Mysteries focus on Jesus' agony in the Garden, scourging at the pillar, crowning with thorns, carrying the cross, and the crucifixion. The Glorious Mysteries focus on the resurrection, the ascension, the descent of the Holy Spirit, the assumption of Mary, and the crowning of Mary as queen of heaven and earth.

As Christians, our lives are to be molded on and fashioned by the life of Jesus, but we cannot imitate what we do not know. By meditating on the mysteries of the rosary, our thoughts and actions can be molded to help us be more Christlike. If praying the rosary is unfamiliar to you, pamphlets and websites can help guide you through the prayers and mysteries. Such aids often include meditations and step-by-step guides.

Saint John Paul II formalized the most recent set of mysteries—the Luminous Mysteries or mysteries of light. In his 2019 book *The 10 Wonders of the Rosary*, Fr. Donald Calloway states, "The Luminous Mysteries shed light on the darkness of modern-day falsehoods." The baptism in the Jordan speaks to the importance of baptism in the life of a Christian. The wedding feast at Cana speaks to the importance and sanctity of marriage. The Sermon on the Mount speaks to the ongoing need for conversion in the life of all Christians. The transfiguration speaks to the divinity of Christ at a time when so many are referring to Jesus as one of many prophets who can lead one to God. The institution of the Eucharist speaks to Christ's Real Presence in holy Communion, which some deny nowadays—even in the Church. Meditating on these and the other mysteries each day helps us become more Christlike and aware of central teachings of our faith.

Most popes and saints through the ages have encouraged the faithful to pray the rosary—for our families, our country, for peace, and the salvation of the world. The truth is, we never run out of reasons to pray the rosary. Saint Padre Pio and others who have had numerous encounters with the evil one speak of the rosary as "a glorious weapon against Satan." In 1917 at Fatima, Portugal, an apparition of our Lady asked that the rosary be prayed to bring about the end of World War I. She also asked it to be prayed for the conversion of communist Russia. In today's world, we need the rosary more than ever to help combat the violence, hatred, division, chaos, and destructive forces of evil all around us.

No prayer, including the rosary, is magic. Praying twenty rosaries will not guarantee your request will be granted. The sacrifice of time and attention is an action of love, and love changes everything. Opening our heart to God through prayer changes us.

Devotion to Mary also changes us, especially when this devotion includes a consecration. Consecration is an entrusting of ourselves to one's particular care, such as Jesus and Mary. Consecration makes or declares someone or something to be sacred. We Catholics consecrate churches, altars, vessels for Mass, bread and wine, and more. Once consecrated the object is sacred. We, on the other hand, are works in progress. Consecration assists us on our journey. According to St. Louis de Montfort, total consecration to Jesus through Mary is the "quickest, easiest, surest way to grow in holiness." Saint Teresa of Calcutta, St. John Paul II, and St. Maximilian Kolbe all stated that their Marian consecrations were transformative moments in their journeys. Saint Thérèse of Lisieux made her consecration to Jesus through Mary on her first holy Communion day. In *Redemptoris Mater* (46), St. John Paul II states:

> For every Christian, for every human being, Mary is the one who first "believed," and precisely with her faith as Spouse and Mother she wishes to act upon all those who entrust themselves to her as her children. And it is well known that the more her children persevere and progress in this attitude, the nearer Mary leads them to the "unsearchable riches of Christ" (Ephesians 3:8).

THE SAINTS

Queen of All Saints is one of the Blessed Mother's more familiar titles. As she was the first to believe in the Incarnation, God coming in human flesh, she is honored with this title. She is our model in faith and holiness and, from her place in heaven, intercedes for us on earth.

Thankfully, many wonderful models of faith and intercessors are in heaven. These are the saints, those recognized by the Church to be men and women of virtue who were either martyred for the gospel message or lived a life of heroic virtue. The Dogmatic Constitution on the Church (*Lumen Gentium*, 49) states:

> By reason of the fact that those in heaven are more closely united with Christ, they establish the whole Church more firmly in holiness....They do not cease to intercede with the Father for us, showing forth the merits which they won on earth through the one Mediator between God and man....Thus by their brotherly interest our weakness is greatly strengthened.

As mentioned, all baptized Catholics are a part of the mystical body of Christ. The body includes those on their journey with God on earth, those in purgatory making their way to the fullness of God's holy presence, and those who are currently in the fullness of the presence of God in heaven. While we Christians might be accustomed to asking one another or our parish priest to pray for us, the Church teaches us that those who share in God's holy presence in heaven now are particularly righteous and find favor with God. In Scripture we find examples of this: "For the eyes of the Lord are on the righteous and his ears turned to their prayer" (1 Peter 3:12). And, "the fervent prayer of a righteous person is very powerful" (James 5:16).

When I'm looking for prayer for a particular need, I'm more likely to call on a friend whom I view as closer to God rather than someone who may not be living a Christian lifestyle. In the same way, I would often call on someone who has some connection to me or my specific need. For example, I more likely would call on another parent to ask for prayers for my son because that person would be more familiar with my current concerns.

In a similar way, we turn to the saints in heaven who may have a particular connection with us or our situation. For example, I was named after St. Thérèse of Lisieux, so I often turn to her for support because I feel a strong connection with her. In a similar way, you might call on St. Monica, the mother of St. Augustine, for her intercession on behalf of your adult child who might be separated from the Church like Augustine was for many years.

Many Christian children are named after a saint. Those who made their confirmation may feel a connection to the saint they chose as a companion on their journey of faith. Most parishes are under the special protection and patronage of a particular saint. As a member of that parish, you also are under that patronage and can call on that saint for intercession.

Saints represent all cultures, languages, vocations (single, married, widowed, religious, and ordained), occupations, and life challenges. Many were mocked and belittled for their faith in God, some suffering death. Saint Elizabeth Ann Seton of the United States was a single mother of five children. Saint Thérèse of France had a family member with mental illness. Saint Anthony of Padua of Portugal was a priest known for reconciling separated couples. Saint Peregrine of Italy is known as the patron saint of those suffering from cancer, AIDS, and other illnesses. As I write this book, I have called on St. Francis de Sales of France—the patron saint of authors and journalists—for assistance. God gives much help on our journey, many forms of grace. All of these have one purpose: to help us unite more closely with him in prayer and in everlasting life.

Many in the body of Christ can help us on our journey with God in prayer, from family and friends to the many saints in heaven—including Jesus' Mother. If we desire to be united with

God in prayer, we have an army ready and waiting to assist.

REFLECTION QUESTIONS

1. *Do you believe that meditating on the life of Jesus, as we do in the rosary, can help us imitate the Lord in love and action?*

2. *Have you seen people who carry or pray a rosary? If so, what does this visual say to you about their faith life?*

3. *What are the four sets of mysteries? Is there one you would be more drawn to pray than the others? Why or why not?*

4. *Are there saints you connect with either by your name, parish, occupation, nationality, or something else? How were you introduced to those saints? Is there a way to allow them to help you in your journey of faith?*

FURTHER READING

Calloway, Donald. *10 Wonders of the Rosary.* Stockbridge, Massachusetts: Marian Press, 2019.

De Montfort, Louis. *True Devotion to Mary: With Preparation for Total Consecration.* Charlotte, North Carolina: TAN Books, 2010.

Hahn, Scott. *Hail Holy Queen: The Mother of God in the Word of God.* New York: Doubleday, 2001.

Zimmer, Mary Ann. *Mary 101: Tradition and Influence.* Liguori, Missouri: Liguori Publications, 2010.

CHAPTER 7

Prayer and the Arts

A picture is worth a thousand words.

FREDERICK R. BARNARD

All of life can be used to connect us to God and, therefore, everything can be an opportunity for prayer. We can see this demonstrated in the lives of the saints. For instance, St. Joseph is the patron of fathers and workers, St. Thérèse of Lisieux is the patron saint of missionaries, St. Matthew is the patron of bookkeepers, and St. Cecilia is the patron of musicians. You can find a patron saint associated with almost any profession or enterprise. This connection between the things we do for employment, recreation, entertainment, and all of life's activities can be forms of prayer because we can open our hearts and minds to God in the process. This can be especially true with the arts.

Our friend Sally is doing well in her relationship with God now and has various ways to connect with him. But there's more. Hanging in her home is an image of Jesus with a muddy lamb on his shoulders. This image had hung in her family home as a child and now resides in her own home. She hasn't looked directly at it for some time, but as her relationship with God develops, she sees it with new eyes. What might this religious image say to her about Jesus and herself? Could it remind her of the Lord's constant care, that he will never abandon her? Is she sometimes like the muddy lamb that needs to be rescued and cleansed from sin?

Similarly, Sally finds herself humming happy tunes all day long. The upbeat numbers she sings keep her connected to happiness and to God. She reminds herself of the joy God gives her each day and the positive energy she experiences just having the gift of life, like the characters in the songs she loves.

Since ancient times, music, dance, and other forms of art have been avenues for people to connect with God. If we were to look at the Jewish Temple in Jerusalem around 957 BC, we would see elaborate carvings on the walls that led people to think of God's promises. In an ancient synagogue, archeologists have found images of Moses and the Israelites crossing the Red Sea, as well as of other significant events in their lives. King David wrote much of the biblical Book of Psalms, a collection of hymns about God. They sing of his goodness, mercy, and faithfulness as well as of the struggles involved with remaining faithful to God in times of trouble. King David, Scripture says, even danced with holy abandon before the Ark of the Covenant, expressing his joy, as it was brought into Jerusalem.

The arts can be channels for our feelings and emotions, such as joy, sorrow, peace, and love. Since God is involved and interested in all aspects of our lives, including our emotions, these expressions can form the connection with God we all seek. That connection is prayer. In discussing art, the *Catechism* says:

> Created "in the image of God," man also expresses the truth of his relationship with God the Creator by the beauty of his artistic works. Indeed, art is a distinctively human form of expression; beyond the search for the necessities of life which is common to all living creatures, art is a freely given superabundance of the human being's inner riches. Arising from talent given by the Creator and from man's own effort, art is a form of practical wisdom, uniting knowledge and skill, to give form to the truth of reality

in a language accessible to sight or hearing. To the extent that it is inspired by truth and love of beings, art bears a certain likeness to God's activity in what he has created. Like any other human activity, art is not an absolute end in itself, but is ordered to and ennobled by the ultimate end of man (*CCC* 2501).

Art "ordered to and ennobled by the ultimate end of man" can easily help us to connect with God. Much art is not ordered specifically to God's glory, yet for the believer, everything can be an avenue to connect with God. There are numerous movies out there with a religious theme, but it was a nonreligious movie, *City Slickers*, that had the greatest impact on my life with God. It was about a middle-aged man, played by Billy Crystal, looking for meaning in his life. He found his meaning in family. The movie led me to ponder that same age-old question. As I explored options of how to find purpose in my life, I realized that by setting my focus and intentions on God, my life would hold eternal meaning. We can use anything to connect with God, as he is always reaching out to connect with us.

Through the ages, art and song have been used to communicate truths about God and help people connect with God. Stained-glass windows, for example, have been used to communicate various scenes from the Bible and other Church teachings. A Church I visited had the mysteries of the rosary depicted in stained glass. While it was beautiful to the eye, it is also easier to remember images than something like a list of the mysteries. Church hymns are also used to express truths of God. Hymns like "On Eagle's Wings" remind us of our future home in heaven. These truths can speak to our heart and help us unite with God in prayer.

In looking more closely at music and art as vehicles for prayer in our lives, I'd like to make a distinction. For our purposes, music and works of art can be understood in three categories: sacred, religious, and secular. Sacred art or music is that which is used in liturgical settings: Mass and the sacraments. Music used in liturgical settings must meet certain guidelines and that it must adhere to Catholic doctrine and add to the nature and purpose of the liturgy (*CCC* 1156–58). The same is true for sacred art displayed in a Catholic church. Religious art or music is that which aids and supports the Christian faith but is not for use in the liturgy, scholars say. Secular art or music does not have a religious theme but can still be an avenue for devotion and worship. An example might be a landscape painting that leads someone to ponder the beauty of God's creation.

MUSIC AND SONG

"He who sings prays twice" is a popular quotation, though there is some question about its origin. Nonetheless, to pray using spoken words is wonderful, but when expressed musically, so much more can be conveyed. Scripture implores us again and again to sing out to the Lord with joyful hymns and songs: "Sing to the LORD a new song; / sing to the LORD, all the earth. / Sing to the LORD, bless his name; / proclaim his salvation day after day. / Tell his glory among the nations; among all peoples, his marvelous deeds" (Psalm 96:1–3). "Sing hymns to the LORD enthroned on Zion" (Psalm 9:12). In his letter to the Ephesians, St. Paul asks that we address "one another [in] psalms and hymns and spiritual songs, singing and playing to the Lord in your hearts" (Ephesians 5:19). Singing as a form of prayer has existed since the earliest days of Judaism, which is at the root of Christianity itself. Much of the Jewish liturgy was sung as a better expression of emotions than mere words. Jesus, participating in the Jewish liturgy, would have himself engaged in song as prayer. The Book of Psalms is itself a book of hymns to be sung. There are even parts that give directions to the musicians, such as in Psalm 61: "For the leader; with stringed instruments."

Music has a way of touching and expressing the very heart of who we are. There are many songs that touch me so deeply that I cry, and others that lift me up so much I feel like I am on cloud nine. Plato, a philosopher from ancient Greece, said, "Rhythm and harmony find their way into the inward places of the soul." I agree.

In addition to speaking to and coming from these deep places in our soul, music helps us learn truths more easily and is used to pass on teachings from one generation to the next. Remember learning your ABCs as a child? They were put to music. What about songs to learn counting or colors? Even adults learn more easily through song. In Moses' time we see the Israelites singing about God's saving work at the parting of the Red Sea. "Then Moses and the Israelites sang this song to the LORD: I will sing to the LORD, for he is gloriously triumphant; horse and chariot he has cast into the sea" (Exodus 15:1). These songs enabled the stories of God's mercy and goodness to be passed between generations, so as not to be forgotten.

There are some forms of music that can be categorized as prayer. Hymns, many of which are a type of sacred music, are songs created to be sung by the congregation to worship God. The word *hymn* comes from the Greek, meaning "song of praise." Hymns are often sung in liturgical settings like Mass and Holy Hours. Many hymns have been published, but only some have been approved for use in the Catholic liturgy. Anyone can write a hymn, but it is the Church's responsibility to assure its doctrine is correct.

Instrumental music can be very prayerful, helping us quiet down and become open to God's presence. It can also be used as background for a time of prayer. It can help to create a peaceful, slower pace for our time with God. Timothy Cardinal Dolan from the Archdiocese of New York said in an interview he likes to use instrumental music as a backdrop during his time of prayer each morning. "I find quiet music renews my weary soul, refreshes me, and leads me to lift my heart to God," he said. Baroque composer Johann Sebastian Bach had this to say: "The aim and final end of all music should be none other than the glory of God and the refreshment of the soul."

Chants are another form of sacred music and prayer. Gregorian chants can be traced back to the seventh century and St. Gregory the Great. Gregorian chants were written to accompany the words of the liturgy, both the Mass and the Divine Office. One reason for their popularity through the centuries is that they do not require instrumental accompaniment. Many religious communities today still chant the Divine Office throughout the day.

The music of Taizé, a town in France, is more recent and is used in prayer services around the world. It is ecumenical in nature, designed to unite Christians of various denominations and encourage them to worship God together. It would be considered religious, not sacred music—though some may be approved for liturgical use. It emphasizes simple phrases, generally taken from Scripture or liturgy and repeated many times. For example, "Jesus, remember me when you come into your kingdom" is a common passage used in prayer services (Luke 23:42). This type of music is considered very contemplative because the words are so simple and repetitive that one can easily settle into a contemplative presence with God amid the words. Some might refer to it as a form of centering prayer.

While much praiseworthy music has been around for thousands of years, new music is always on the scene. I'm talking about contemporary Christian music. This category includes songs from genres like country, folk, pop, dance, rap, rock, and others. In general, contemporary Christian would be considered religious music, though some has been included in the realm of sacred music approved for liturgical use. These songs have a current feel but speak of God, his mercies, his ways, and how to live the gospel message. Some of the songs are based on sacred Scripture, while others center on personal experiences. I credit much of my early growth in the faith to listening to Christian music. It helped me consider and ponder the truths of my faith in an upbeat way accompanied by catchy tunes. I was repeatedly fed the gospel message through various artists who kept me from listening to secular music that was focused on worldly, and at times, sinful things.

"Praise and Worship" is a category that falls within the heading of contemporary Christian music. This type of music is not so much about God and living out the message as it is focused on God himself. These tunes sing his praises and glorify him. I compare it to telling my son how great he is rather than telling others about our relationship. Some of these songs have also been approved for use in the liturgy. Many are directly or indirectly taken from the Book of Psalms. Since they are enmeshed with God's word, they create in the singer and listener an encounter with God. These songs also fed me spiritually at the beginning of my faith journey and play a major role in my journey today. For me, music makes St. Paul's directive "to pray always" much easier to accomplish. In sadness or joy, music is one of my favorite prayer forms.

VISUAL ARTS

What music can do through hearing, paintings and sculpture can do through vision. Every image can help us connect to God in prayer. A picture of suffering can lead to compassion and prayers for those who suffer. An image of an innocent and pure child can likewise evoke a connection with God. This is true with almost any image, religious or secular. As mentioned, either a landscape or an image from Scripture can speak of God. He is not limited to things strictly religious, though religious images can make it easier to make those connections. Leonardo da Vinci's *The Last Supper* or Michelangelo's frescos in the Sistine Chapel can communicate truths of God to some people more easily than, say, something by Monet.

A picture can convey different meanings to different people. I can look at a photograph and maybe the beautiful landscape catches my attention, speaking to me of God's beauty and goodness. It may even lead to feelings of gratitude, to have eyes to see it. Another person may look on that same image and they see a house in the foreground with two people sitting on a porch. The image may communicate companionship and providence to that person, who may not even notice the dramatic landscape. When God speaks, he does so to the individual, fully aware of one's needs and concerns.

Devotional images have been found in the homes of Christians for many centuries. Growing up, I would see an image of Jesus or the Blessed Mother in almost every home I visited. Today, I have devotional images in my home. While I don't often stop to pray and meditate with each one, I find that having the images around helps me to turn my mind and heart to God throughout my day. Catching a glimpse of a statue of the Blessed Mother might remind me on a particularly difficult day that our Lady is praying for me. Noticing a crucifix in another room can remind me of the role suffering plays in love and life. An image of Elijah, an Old Testament prophet, can remind me to take time to be quiet, as God usually speaks softly.

Gazing or meditating on an image may be enough for you to connect with God. For those looking for additional help in making those connections, the practice of *visio divina* may be helpful. Remember, *lectio divina* is a way of holy reading. *Visio divina,* with its simple prayerful steps, is similar. In *visio divina,* you take an image, religious or secular, and settle in a quiet place, opening your heart to God. Then prayerfully gaze upon the image, looking at what it depicts: the scene, the colors, the lighting, the background and foreground, and then rest quietly. Look at the image again, this time noting what catches your attention. Allow God to speak to you through that part of the image. Sit quietly with this message. Gaze again upon the image and let yourself rest in God's presence. This practice of *visio divina* can also be done with a particular Bible passage that the image may directly or indirectly depict. The practice may be done alone or in groups.

Colors play a major role in much art, often used to express emotions and meaning. The artist's choice of color for a person's clothing, the sky, a building's walls, and more all communicate something of her or his message. This is especially true in iconography. An *icon*, Greek for "image," is art whose primary goal is to connect people who view it with God. Icons follow certain rules about the use of colors, symbols, and hand gestures that all help the viewer to connect with the Divine. The artist's use of hues follows a kind of "theology of colors," as each color communicates various truths of the faith. For example, the color gold speaks of the eternal, uncreated light of God. White represents heavenly purity. Icons of the resurrection often show Jesus in a white robe. White is also used for angels and babies. Icons also use images, hand gestures, and lettering to communicate meaning, forming an artistic language. For this reason, it is said that icons are "written" rather than painted.

Icons are often called "windows to the Divine." When gazing at an icon, take notice of the eyes. They appear to look back at you. Iconologists and others say this is because, through an icon, viewers can see into heaven and be seen in a special way.

Through this experience, the viewer connects with God. Icons often are of Jesus, Mary, or a saint, though they can depict a Bible scene. While the artistic qualities of icons are beautiful, the artist or "writer" does not seek for the "reader" (the person gazing on the image) to admire his artistic skills, but to look beyond the image toward God. For this reason, icons are not generally signed by the artist.

Many people connect with God through art created by others. Many artists create works as an expression of their faith. Creating art connects them to God. But this act of connecting with God through artistic creativity is not reserved for skilled artists alone.

Although I possess little artistic talent, art gives me an avenue to express myself to God when words seem inadequate. God creates our emotions and seeks to connect with us through them. I may be bursting with joy or in the depths of pain and sorrow, yet God is there. At times I connect with God and my emotions through abstract drawing or doodling. I begin by opening my heart to God, then speak to him through colors and shapes. Even the pressure I place on my pencil or crayon communicates something of my emotional state. I've even been known to "scream" out my deepest frustrations and pain to God in this way. In moments of joy, I may fill the page with yellows and pinks, while in moments of pain I may choose duller colors like muted reds, grays, and black. I'm not solely expressing my emotions. I'm connecting with God in prayer; the God who loves me unconditionally and wants to touch me with his love and healing presence.

NATURE

"Beauty is God's handwriting," said Ralph Waldo Emerson. Though we've seen how this beauty can be expressed through music or the visual arts, it is most perfectly expressed through nature. A painting of a sunset can seek to capture its radiance, but it often falls short. Human artfulness is a dim reflection of God's beauty. God is the ultimate artist!

While being in touch with nature can renew and refresh us, it becomes prayer when we are present to the presence of God revealed in nature. Nature itself is not God! Believing that is idolatry. Nature draws our attention to the Creator to give him glory and recognize the many truths of who he is. When we see how God cares for birds, nature reveals God's loving care (Matthew 6:26). God's power is revealed in the thunder of a raging river. His beauty is revealed in the structure of a flower. His creativity is seen in the intricacy of a spider's web. And, to quote Pope Francis, "You are called to care for creation not only as responsible citizens but as followers of Christ."

"Never will I forget the impression the sea made upon me," writes St. Thérèse of Lisieux in *The Story of a Soul*, her autobiography. "I couldn't take my eyes off it since its majesty, the roaring of its waves, everything spoke to my soul of God's grandeur and power." All of creation, the mountains, the seas, the animals, the flowers—yes, all of it—sings the glory of God. Recognizing God's self-revelation through nature can lead us to sing his praises and to be filled with awe at his magnificence. This, too, is prayer.

One day while on retreat, I walked down a path meditating on how I was made in the image of God. I came upon a doe with her fawn. As we both stood looking at the other, I remembered how I used to point out the beauty of God revealed in the deer to my young son. Then I imagined the deer saying to its fawn: *Oh look, little one. That is a human made in the image of God. Isn't she amazing?* Through this I realized more fully the blessing I received in being not just one of God's many creations, but that I was made in his image. Gazing on creation can lead us to lift our minds and hearts to God, but it is also an opportunity for God to speak to us in stillness, a gentle breeze, or a refreshing rain shower.

God uses anything and everything to speak to us. We also can be creative in how we speak to God, and all of this is prayer. God is present with us in every moment of every day waiting for us to recognize him and share a whisper of love.

REFLECTION QUESTIONS

1. *Was a devotional image or statue displayed in your home when your were growing up? If so, what was it and did it hold any meaning for you?*

2. *The cross of Christ is often depicted in religious art. Why do you think that is?*

3. *The Book of Psalms is a collection of hymns to God. In your Bible or online, look up Psalms 23 and 33. What are they about? How might these hymns speak to you today?*

4. *Has a movie, secular or religious, affected your journey with God? If so, explain.*

5. *At Mass on Sundays, we sing hymns and other parts of the Mass. Does singing at Mass add to your experience and facilitate an encounter with God?*

6. *Is there a hymn or contemporary Christian song that helps you to connect with God? If so, what song is it and what is it about?*

7. *Saint John Paul II was known for his love of nature and was often seen praying on mountaintops and along wooded paths. What role does nature play in your ability to connect with God?*

CHAPTER 8

Praying with the Holy Spirit

Christian missionary Samuel Zwemer (1867–1952) said, "True prayer is God the Holy Spirit talking to God the Father in the name of God the Son, and the believer's heart is the prayer room." While I never like the designation "true prayer," Zwemer's words led me to reflect more fully on the role of the Holy Spirit in our prayer lives.

We receive the Holy Spirit at baptism, and confirmation completes the action begun at baptism: the full outpouring of the Holy Spirit into our lives (see *CCC* 1302–04). So, what role does the Holy Spirit play in our lives? I think most people are more accustomed to thinking about and praying to Jesus and God the Father, but the Holy Spirit? Not as much.

Fr. Raniero Cantalamessa, preacher to the papal household, once commented that the Holy Spirit is poured like chocolate syrup into milk. It is in the milk, but it just rests there, not mixing with the milk—changing it or transforming it—until it is stirred. Then all the milk is changed and transformed. Many Catholics today have the Holy Spirit but have not really experienced this stirring, allowing the Holy Spirit to bring life to all we do. The Nicene Creed we pray aloud at Mass says the Holy Spirit is "the Lord, the giver of life." And yet we struggle to understand who he is and the role he plays in our lives. Have you ever received a gift from someone and forgot to open it? This is a great example of the relationship some people have with the

Holy Spirit—an unopened gift. When we Catholics make the sign of the cross, we simultaneously pray, "In the name of the Father, and of the Son, and of the Holy Spirit" before we begin our next prayer. But we may pray the words of the Sign of the Cross with little awareness of its meaning. For instance, what does it mean to pray "in the name...of the Holy Spirit"?

The Holy Spirit is the third person of the Trinity, with God the Father first and the Son second. Does this mean he is any less God than the Father or the Son? No. The Church teaches that the Holy Spirit is the love that flows between the Father and the Son, and that love dwells within us. In the Book of John, Jesus promises to send the Holy Spirit to be with us always (14:16–18). Saint John Paul II wrote that "through the Holy Spirit, the Father and the Son come to him [the baptized] and take up their abode with him" (On the Holy Spirit in the Life of the Church and the World *[Dominum et vivificantem]*, 58). So, Jesus promises to send the Holy Spirit to help us on our journey, with the Holy Spirit coming to us through our baptism. Pope Francis encourages us to "...learn to invoke the Holy Spirit more often!" Saint Paul implores us to "be filled with the Holy Spirit" (Ephesians 5:18), who is—as St. John Paul II's encyclical reminds us—"the Lord and giver of life."

THE ROLE OF THE HOLY SPIRIT

How does the Holy Spirit help us? John's Gospel is quite direct about this: "Without me you can do nothing" (15:5). The Holy Spirit's role is to sanctify (make holy) the Church, which is the people of God. Thus, if we are unable to grow in holiness, that is because our relationship with God is lacking the Holy Spirit.

The Holy Spirit is present in our lives to help us to grow in holiness, but how? The Spirit enables us to recognize that Jesus is Lord (see 1 Corinthians 12:3). During the days Jesus walked the earth, many people met him and heard him preach, but many did not recognize him as the Messiah. Today, many people know of Jesus but do not recognize him as God. Why? People can only see the truth of Jesus as God through the power of the Holy Spirit. We must fully allow the Holy Spirit to be in us.

The Holy Spirit brings with him his many gifts, including wisdom, understanding, counsel, fortitude, knowledge, piety, and fear of God. These gifts enable us to reject sin and choose rightly according to God and his ways. The Spirit also gives us a "spirit of sonship," the recognition that we are children of God. This allows us to call God our Father. It is this spirit of sonship that gives us courage to even approach the throne of God, recognize his desire, and call to us to be his daughters and sons. Without the Holy Spirit, we might feel that calling on God would be like asking a stranger for a favor.

PRAYING WITH OTHERS AND HEALING PRAYER

As members of the mystical body of Christ, we are called to connect with God personally and to reach out and be Christ to others. We spoke about Sally wanting to pray for her friend who was struggling with her teen daughter. This is being Christ to another. So, Sally goes home and prays for her friend privately. Matthew 18:20 tells us that "where two or three are gathered in my name, there am I in the midst of them." What if Sally, right there in the middle of the supermarket, invited her friend to pray? Her friend, if she agreed to it, would probably feel strengthened, supported, and blessed. What would Sally say? In my earlier days, when this type of prayer seemed foreign to me, I would listen closely to others as they prayed aloud. I would even practice at home in case the Lord called on me to pray in a moment like this. When the moment first came, and every time since, it was the Holy Spirit who guided me. And, while I stumbled a few times, the grace of the moment was almost tangible. The Gospel of Mark assures us, "Say whatever will be given to you at that hour. For it will not be you who are speaking but the holy Spirit" (13:11).

Throughout the New Testament, we read how the disciples, filled with the Holy Spirit, went about praying with people: for their conversion, healing, deliverance, or whatever their needs were. These prayers, prayed in the power of the Holy Spirit, transformed people's lives. Prayer is not just for us as individuals, or even for us to intercede for others while in the privacy of our own homes, but to bring the power of prayer to the marketplace, to the ballfield, to work, and to school. Our world is so wounded and desperately in need of God's healing. This healing can come in the form of physical, mental, emotional, and spiritual healing, but also as deliverance, wisdom, hope, love, and so much more. The Holy Spirit brings those gifts to us so we, God's partners in prayer, can bring his healing to our hurting world.

Before I go further on this topic of praying for healing, please note it is very important to seek professional help first for all illness: physical, mental, and emotional. At the same time, bring it to God. There is no reason to wait and see if professional help works before bringing your need to God. Most often, God heals through conventional means. When a physician diagnoses your health issue and offers a remedy, this is through the healing power of God. It is not just doctors or God, but God through the doctors. Doctors are God's vessels for healing. Even the ability of a body to regenerate and heal itself is God's action.

At times, God heals through miraculous means. This can come in sacramental form through the sacraments of reconciliation or the anointing of the sick. But it can also come in nonsacramental form. Within the Church are many who have sought and seek healing by going on pilgrimage to places known for miraculous healings, such as Lourdes, France. The healing waters of Lourdes have been a vessel of God's healing since the spring was discovered after St. Bernadette saw a vision of the Blessed Mother in 1858. Others have received miraculous healing through the intercession of various saints. For a person to be canonized in the Catholic Church, two verifiable miracles must be attributed to his or her intercession. These miracles are almost always in the form of physical healings.

Scripture illustrates the use of prayer for healing. Psalm 107 is a request to God for healing: "In their distress they cried to the LORD, / who saved them in their peril, / Sent forth his word to heal them, / and snatched them from the grave" (107:19–20), as is Psalm 41: "The LORD sustains him on his sickbed" (41:4). In Matthew we find Jesus healing: "His fame spread to all of Syria, and they brought to him all who were sick with various diseases and racked with pain, those who were possessed, lunatics, and paralytics, and he cured them" (4:24). Also in that Gospel we read: "Great crowds came to him, having with them the lame, the blind, the deformed, the mute, and many others. They placed them at his feet, and he cured them" (Matthew 15:30). In Luke, Jesus sends his disciples, saying, "Whatever town you enter and they welcome you, eat what is set before you, cure the sick in it and say to them, 'The kingdom of God is at hand for you,'" (10:8–9). In the Acts of the Apostles, we read: "After this had taken place, the rest of the sick on the island came to Paul and were cured" (28:9).

From the very beginning of Christianity, bringing healing to a hurting world has been central to its ministry and purpose. This healing that Jesus, and then the disciples, brought to the people of their time served a greater purpose than the health of single individuals. Scripture tells us many came to believe in Jesus through healings and other miracles (see Luke 7:15–17, Matthew 15:31, Acts 9:34–35). When someone is healed, the gift of healing can reach far beyond one person to those who hear of it, so they too may believe in Jesus.

Some people struggle with the idea of God healing today, in the twenty-first century. One reason for this is that it seems not all are healed. When we pray with someone so he or she may receive God's healing, it is important to remain open for the healing God chooses to send. At times he chooses to send the physical healing a person seeks to cure cancer, blood disorders, or blindness. At other times, though, the healing he sends is deeper—perhaps of an emotional or spiritual nature. The key in prayers for healing is to surrender to what God wills. We are only a vessel for God. His love for the person we pray with is far greater than ours. Scripture supports this: "Which one of you would hand his son a stone when he asks for a loaf of bread, or a snake when he asks for a fish? If you then, who are wicked, know how to give good gifts to your children, how much more will your heavenly Father give good things to those who ask him" (Matthew 7:9–11). To ask God for healing and trust him with the results is to express our faith and trust in him who gives us our very life.

SURRENDER, THE MORE PERFECT PRAYER

Being open to the healing God often requires us to surrender to his will instead of clinging tightly to what we believe is best. This mindset does not come naturally to us. It requires God's grace, which is the fruit of prayer. Consider this scenario. Sally's husband, Steve, after developing a wonderful prayer life, learns his only kidney is failing. He seeks the Lord's healing both in the sacraments and through the prayers of friends and relatives. His diagnosis remains unchanged. Though Steve would love to be healed and go about his life with his family, he chooses to remain open to what God has planned for him amid this struggle. When he visits the doctor, he is told he must undergo dialysis. As he goes for regular treatments, he becomes friendly with a few of the people at the dialysis center. During their conversations, Steve begins sharing with them all the Lord has done for him, piquing the interest of Joe, who has been away from the Church since he was a teen. Through their conversations, Joe decides to rededicate his life to God. Unfortunately, they both lose their earthly battle. But because of Steve's presence in the dialysis center and his sharing with Joe, they are both welcomed into God's glorious presence. Steve's surrender during this struggle enabled God to use him. Had he not accepted this difficult direction, Steve may have himself become bitter and frustrated, potentially even turning his own back on God.

Surrendering to God's will is rarely easy. In the Garden of Gethsemane, we see Jesus struggling with this: "He advanced a little and fell prostrate in prayer, saying, 'My Father, if it is possible, let this cup pass from me; yet, not as I will, but as you will'" (Matthew 26:39). Additionally, in the Our Father, Jesus teaches us to pray, "Thy will be done" (see Matthew 6:10). God will use every situation to draw his children near to him. This is the greatest desire of God's heart. He "wills everyone to be saved and to come to knowledge of the truth" (1 Timothy 2:4).

Remember, our prayers begin with gestures and the words of the Sign of the Cross: "In the name of the Father, and of the Son, and of the Holy Spirit." To pray in the name of the Father, Son, and Holy Spirit involves praying with God who works within us and acknowledging that God knows what is best in every situation. "We do not know how to pray as we ought, but the Spirit itself intercedes" (Romans 8:26). Without the Holy Spirit working in our lives, we would be praying for things contrary to the will of God. We generally desire what *we* judge to be best. But because of our fallen nature, we might not recognize what *is* best in a situation. Yet as a child wants ice cream before a nutritious dinner, we, the children of God, are not the best judge of what is best for us. "Oh God, please let me get this job!" someone might pray. What if God has a better job or opportunity waiting for you—one with better pay and benefits, and allows you more time with your family? Do you want the first job, the one you can see? Or do you want the best God has for us? When we pray in God's name, we accept his will.

Our Lady, our model of prayer, prayed this way when the angel Gabriel came to her and told her she would bear the Messiah. "Mary said, 'Behold, I am the handmaid of the Lord. May it be done to me according to your word.' Then the angel departed from her" (Luke 1:38). Mary surrendered to what God willed in her life. She did not understand what this surrender would entail, but her trust in God empowered her to give herself freely to him in all circumstances. For Mary, as for us, this *fiat* (let it be done) is a powerful prayer.

Along these lines is the theme of one of my favorite books, *The Sacrament of the Present Moment*, by Jean-Pierre de Caussade (1675–1751), a Jesuit priest. This 100-page book tells how God reveals his will for us in each moment of each day. For example, if it rains on a picnic, then that can be seen as God's will for the moment. God is Creator of the universe, and nothing can happen in our lives that he has not, in some way—either directly or through his permissive will—sanctioned for his purposes. Sometimes this approach to prayer and surrender can be difficult to understand, especially in times of pain and sorrow. Yet, like the prophet Job, we can meet God in all of it.

THE PRAYER OF RECOLLECTION

This final aspect of prayer to consider is a style of prayer that comes from the writings of many prayer masters in the Church, including Teresa of Ávila, John of the Cross, and Thérèse of Lisieux. They each speak of it a bit differently, but all have the same common element: to always be aware and attentive to God's presence in us and around us, and to be united with God in a holy union.

Br. Lawrence of the Resurrection (1614–91), a Carmelite, was a simple man whose duties involved mundane kitchen tasks. *The Practice of the Presence of God* is a collection of his writings and conversations. In them he speaks about a way of prayer where he holds firmly to the truth that God is ever present and therefore we can pray by turning our attention to him. Scripture affirms this, stating, "In him we live and move and have our being" (Acts 17:28). Br. Lawrence believed that prayer could be as simple as a glance inward, noticing God with the eyes of his heart. It does not require special holy places or mountaintop experiences; a simple glance united him with God in each moment. Some describe this as a practiced habit of being with God.

In a similar way, St. Elizabeth of the Trinity (1880–1906), a Carmelite nun canonized in 2016, wrote of living each day, each moment abiding with the indwelling Holy Trinity: Father, Son, and Holy Spirit. "It seems to me I have found heaven on earth, since heaven is God, and God is in my soul," she wrote in a letter. If asked, people will usually say they want to go to heaven, but they may not consider the truth of what heaven is: being with God. He is the one who designed prayer to prepare and transform us for the life to come. Indeed a shadow of the fullness of heaven that awaits us is present in our world today.

Prayers of healing, surrender, and recollection are all prayers of trust in God's unfailing mercy. God, despite our failings and faults, wants only the best for us, his beloved. When we can remember this great truth, we realize there is nothing—even allowing the death of his own Son—he wouldn't do to have us spend forever with him!

REFLECTION QUESTIONS

1. *What is the main role of the Holy Spirit? Do you see the actions of the Holy Spirit in your life or in those around you? What about over the past five or ten years?*

2. *Why is the spirit of sonship (male and female) important in the Christian life?*

3. *How can praying with someone in the moment affect the person leading the prayer? The person being prayed for? Witnesses to this prayer?*

4. *Why is it important for a person who receives healing to share her or his experience with others?*

5. *How might God's purposes have been fulfilled by the story of Steve and Joe?*

6. *What does the prayer of recollection involve? How might it change one's life?*

FURTHER READING

Br. Lawrence of the Resurrection. *The Practice of the Presence of God.* Mansfield Centre, Connecticut: Martino Publishing, 2016.

De Caussade, Jean-Pierre. *Sacrament of the Present Moment.* New York: Harper & Row Publishers, 1982.

Guitton, Jean. *The Spiritual Genius of St. Thérèse.* Chicago: Triumph Books, 1997.

Korn, Daniel. *Embracing the Icon of Love.* Liguori, Missouri: Liguori Publications, 2015.

MacNutt, Francis. *The Practice of Healing Prayer: A How-to Guide for Catholics.* Frederick, Maryland: The Word Among Us Press, 2010.

Philippe, Jacques. *In the School of the Holy Spirit.* New York: Sceptor Publishers Inc., 2007.

Simsic, Wayne. *Seeking the Beloved: A Prayer Journey with John of the Cross.* Frederick, Maryland: The Word Among Us Press, 2012.

Thérèse of Lisieux. *The Story of a Soul: The Autobiography of St. Thérèse of Lisieux.* Washington, DC: ICS Publications, 1996.

Connecting with God

I was speaking with my adult nephew the other day and dared to ask him how his relationship with God and his prayer life were going. He spoke openly about who God was for him. Though articulating it took some effort, he stuck with it. The conversation ended with me praying with him for an upcoming exam. "You know, no one ever asked me about this before," he said in gratitude. "It was nice to talk about it." I believe most people, while hesitant and unsure of how to do so, are eager to join a conversation about their prayer life and their overall life with God.

Throughout these chapters I spoke about just that in providing a vocabulary that allows us to think of and understand prayer. I examined traditional and conversational types of prayer. I explored meditation and contemplation, as well as praying with Scripture, art, music, nature, and more. I then took a look at praying with the Holy Spirit and what it means to surrender to God's will in our prayer and in our lives.

My goal in this book has been to help you explore various ways to connect with our loving God—Father, Son, and Holy Spirit—who invites us to the joys of eternal life. Eternal life is not reserved for the afterlife. As John says, "Now this is eternal life: that they know you, the only true God, and Jesus Christ, whom you have sent" (17:3). To pray is to know God, to draw close to him who loves you and wants to bless you always.

My prayer now is for you to grow in relationship with our loving God, and from that relationship to be energized and strengthened in love and compassion to bring the message of salvation, the joy of a life lived with God, to your family, friends, neighbors, and all the world. As one of the options for the closing prayer at Mass says, "Go and announce the Gospel of the Lord." May God's peace be with you always!

"It is prayer that transforms this day into grace, or better, that transforms us: it quells anger, sustains love, multiplies joy, instills the strength to forgive."

POPE FRANCIS
GENERAL AUDIENCE
FEBRUARY 10, 2021

Bibliography

Beale, Stephanie. "The Biblical Roots of the Sign of the Cross." Catholic Exchange, 2013. Catholicexchange.com/biblical-roots-sign-cross.

Beliefnet. "7 Ways Christian Meditation Differs From Eastern Religions." 2019. Beliefnet.com/faiths/christianity/galleries/7-ways-christian-meditation-differs-from-eastern-religions.aspx.

Bible Gateway. "Pray." Accessed June 11, 2020. Biblegateway.com/quicksearch/?quicksearch=pray version=NABRE.

Bible Gateway. "Love." Accessed June 11, 2020. Biblegateway.com/quicksearch/?quicksearch=love&version=NABRE.

Br. Lawrence. *Writings and Conversations on the Practice of the Presence of God*. Translated by Salvatore Sciurba. Washington, DC: ICS Publications, 1994.

Brune, Chris. "The Art of Praying With Art." Catholic Stand, 2017. Catholicstand.com/art-praying-art/.

Bussen, Therese. "What Is Consecration and Why Do It?" *Denver Catholic*, 2017. Denvercatholic.org/what-is-consecration-and-why-do-it/.

Calloway, Donald. *10 Wonders of the Rosary*. Stockbridge, Massachusetts: Marian Press, 2019.

Catez, Elizabeth. *The Complete Works of Elizabeth of the Trinity, Vol. 1, I Have Found God*. Translated by Alethia Kane. Washington, DC: ICS Publications, 1984.

Catholic Apologetics. "The Holy Rosary." Accessed February 25, 2021. Catholicapologetics.info/apologetics/general/HolyRsry.htm.

Catholic Church. *Catechism of the Catholic Church*. 2nd ed. Washington, DC: United States Catholic Conference, 2011. Usccb.org/beliefs-and-teachings/what-webelieve/catechism/catechism-of-the-catholic-church/epub/index.cfm.

Chalmers, Joseph. *Mary the Contemplative*. Rome: Edizioni Carmelitane, 2001.

De Caussade, Jean-Pierre. *Sacrament of the Present Moment.* Translated by Kitty Muggeridge. San Francisco: HarperSanFrancisco, 1981.

Della Croce, Giovanna. *Elizabeth of the Trinity: A Life of Praise to God.* Manchester, New Hampshire: Sophia Institute Press, 2016.

Dubay, Thomas. *Fire Within: St. Teresa of Ávila, St. John of the Cross, and the Gospel—on Prayer.* San Francisco: Ignatius Press, 1989.

Green, Thomas H. *Opening to God: A Guide to Prayer.* Notre Dame, Indiana: Ave Maria Press, 2006.

Guitton, Jean. *The Spiritual Genius of St. Thérèse.* Liguori, Missouri: Liguori Publications, 1997.

Hahn, Scott and Regis Flaherty. *Catholic for a Reason III: Scripture and the Mystery of the Mass.* Steubenville, Ohio: Emmaus Road Publishing, 1998.

Hahn, Scott. *Signs of Life, 20 Catholic Customs and their Biblical Roots.* New York: Image, 2018.

Hardesty, Nicholas. "Praying to the Saints." Saint Paul Street Evangelization, 2013. Streetevangelization.com/praying-to-the-saints/.

Hebert, Albert J. *A Prayerbook of Favorite Litanies: 116 Catholic Litanies and Responsory Prayers.* Rockford, Illinois: TAN Books, 1985.

Kavanaugh, Kieran and Rodríguez, Otilio. "The Book of Her Life," essay in *The Collected Works of St. Teresa of Ávila 1.* Washington, DC: Institute of Carmelite Studies, 1987.

Kent, William. "Indulgences." *The Catholic Encyclopedia*, 2019. Newadvent.org/cathen/07783a.htm.

Korn, Daniel. *Embracing the Icon of Love.* Liguori, Missouri: Liguori Publications, 2015.

Liguori, Alphonsus. *The Glories of Mary*, e-catholic 2000. Ecatholic2000.com/liguori/glories15.shtml.

Loyola Press. "How Catholics Pray, Expressions of Prayer." Accessed July 2018. Loyolapress.com/catholic-resources/prayer/personal-prayer-life/different-ways-to-pray/how-catholics-pray/.

MacNutt, Francis. *The Practice of Healing Prayer: A How-to Guide for Catholics.* Frederick, Maryland: The Word Among Us Press, 2010.

Martin, Therese. "Saint Thérèse of the Child Jesus to Sr. Marie Guerin (Celine)." Archives Du Carmel Lisieux, May 30, 1889, Letter 92. Archives-carmel-lisieux.fr/english/carmel/index.php/lt-91-a-100/1096-lt-92-a-marie-guerin.

McBride, Denis. *Praying the Rosary: A Journey through Scripture and Art.* Liguori, Missouri: Liguori Publications, 2014.

Miller, George (director). *Happy Feet.* Burbank, California: Warner Home Video, 2007.

Miller, Michael J. *Youcat English: Youth Catechism of the Catholic Church.* San Francisco: Ignatius Press, 2011.

Miravalle, Mark. *Meet Your Mother: A Brief Introduction to Mary.* Stockbridge, Masschusetts: Marian Press, 2014.

Mullins, Rich. "Awesome God," track three, *On Winds of Heaven, Stuff of Earth.* Reunion Records, Inc., 1988, CD.

Nouwen, Henri J. M. *Behold the Beauty of the Lord: Praying with Icons.* Notre Dame, Indiana: Ave Maria Press, 1987.

Olmstead, Thomas. "Singing the Mass." Adoremus, 2012. Adoremus.org/2012/05/singing-the-mass.

Pable, Martin W. *Prayer: A Practical Guide.* Chicago: ACTA Publications, 2002.

Saint John Paul II. Apostolic Exhortation on the Church in America (*Ecclesia in America*). January 22, 1999. Vatican.va/content/john-paul-ii/en/apost_exhortations/documents/hf_jp-ii_exh_22011999_ecclesia-in-america.html.

Saint John Paul II. Encyclical on the Blessed Virgin Mary in the life of the Pilgrim Church (*Redemptoris Mater*). March 25, 1987. Vatican.va/content/john-paul-ii/en/encyclicals/documents/hf_jp-ii_enc25031987_redemptoris-mater.html.

Saint John Paul II. Encyclical on the Permanent Validity of the Church's Missionary Mandate (*Redemptoris Missio*). December 7, 1990. Vatican.va/content/john-paul-ii/en/encyclicals/documents/hf_jp-ii_enc07121990_redemptoris-missio.html.

Saint John Paul II. Apostolic Letter on the Most Holy Rosary (*Rosarium Virginis Mariae*). March 25, 2021. Vatican.va/content/john-paul-ii/en/apost_letters/2002/documents/hf_jp-ii_apl_20021016_rosarium-virginis-mariae.html.

Saint Paul VI. Encyclical on the Holy Eucharist (*Mysterium Fidei*). September 3, 1965. Vatican.va/content/paul-vi/en/encyclicals/documents/hf_p-vi_enc_03091965_mysterium.html.

Saint Paul VI. Apostolic Letter on the Credo of the People of God (*Solemni Hac Liturgi*). June 30, 1968.
Vatican.va/content/paul-vi/en/motu_proprio/documents/hf_p-vi_motu-proprio_19680630_credo.html.

Randolph, Francis. *Knowing Him in the Breaking of the Bread.* San Francisco: Ignatius Press, 1998.

Redman, Matthew. "10,000 Reasons," track four on *10,000 Reasons.* Kingsway Music, 2011, CD.

Second Vatican Council. Constitution on the Sacred Liturgy (*Sacrosanctum Concilium*). December 4, 1963.

Vatican.va/archive/hist_councils/ii_vatican_council/documents/vat-ii_const_19631204_sacrosanctum-concilium_en.html.

Second Vatican Council. Dogmatic Constitution on the Church (*Lumen Gentium*). November 21, 1964.
Vatican.va/archive/hist_councils/ii_vatican_council/documents/vat-ii_const_19641121_lumen-gentium_en.html.

Sri, Edward. "Getting More Out of the Mass." *Catholic Update.* Liguori, Missouri. January 2017.

Strand, Emily. *Mass 101: Liturgy and Life.* Liguori, Missouri: Liguori Publications, 2013.

US Conference of Catholic Bishops. "Stations of the Cross," 2003. Usccb.org/prayer-and-worship/prayers-and-devotions/stations-of-the-cross/index.cfm.

Traditional Catholic Prayers*

SIGN OF THE CROSS

In the name of the Father,
and of the Son,
and of the Holy Spirit. Amen.

THE OUR FATHER

Our Father, who art in heaven,
hallowed be thy name;
thy kingdom come;
thy will be done on earth as it is in heaven.
Give us this day our daily bread;
and forgive us our trespasses
as we forgive those who trespass against us;
and lead us not into temptation,
but deliver us from evil. Amen.

THE HAIL MARY

Hail Mary, full of grace, the Lord is with thee.
blessed art thou among women,
and blessed is the fruit of thy womb, Jesus.
Holy Mary, Mother of God,
pray for us sinners now and at the hour of our death. Amen.

GLORY BE (DOXOLOGY)

Glory be to the Father, and to the Son, and to the Holy Spirit,
as it was in the beginning, is now, and ever shall be,
world without end. Amen.

THE APOSTLES' CREED

I believe in God,
    the Father almighty,
    Creator of heaven and earth,
    and in Jesus Christ, his only Son, our Lord,
    who was conceived by the Holy Spirit,
    born of the Virgin Mary,
    suffered under Pontius Pilate,
    was crucified, died and was buried;
    he descended into hell;
    on the third day he rose again from the dead;
    he ascended into heaven,
    and is seated at the right hand of God the Father almighty;
    from there he will come to judge the living and the dead.

I believe in the Holy Spirit,
    the holy catholic Church,
    the communion of saints,
    the forgiveness of sins,
    the resurrection of the body,
    and life everlasting. Amen.

GRACE BEFORE MEALS

Bless us, O Lord, and these thy gifts, which we are about to receive from thy bounty, through Christ our Lord. Amen.

ANGEL OF GOD

Angel of God, my guardian dear, to whom God's love commits me here, ever this day be at my side, to light and guard, rule and guide. Amen.

* Source: US Conference of Catholic Bishops

DAILY EXAMENS

The Daily Examen Prayer (A)

1. Become aware of God's presence. Look back on the day and note the times you felt God was with you, assisting. Feel God with you now and ask to become more conscious of God's presence. It may be helpful to repeat a phrase like, "Be still and know that I am God" (Psalm 46:11), or any other prayer that connects you to God.

2. Look back with gratitude. Review the past twenty-four hours and notice what you're thankful for. What happened to make you feel blessed? Take a moment to give thanks to God for providing you with these blessings.

3. Take an honest look at your day. Note everything that happened over the course of the past twenty-four hours, your interactions with others, and your emotions. We often rush though each day, not pausing to reflect. Doing a deep, honest reflection of the past day causes us to learn more about ourselves and improve our future actions.

4. Choose one part of the day and pray about it. From doing your review, you might find something God is directing you to work on—an emotion, a relationship that needs mending, an unpleasant situation. Pray for it, ask God's guidance to resolve it.

5. Pray for tomorrow. Ask God to guide you tomorrow, leading you to your highest purpose. Send love and light to tomorrow, praying for wisdom and strength. Feel deep gratitude, knowing

God has already answered your prayer and tomorrow is already blessed. Take some deep breaths and know that all is well.

Or...

The Daily Examen Prayer (B)

A five-question Examen:
Where did I see God today?
What am I thankful for today?
What did I feel or experience today?
What should I pray for?
How do I feel about tomorrow?

SAMPLE CATHOLIC PRAYER APPS

Bread 4 Today—Offers short meditations for each day. Free.

Hallow—Offers ways to pray, meditations, Scripture study, music, and more. Free and subscription versions are available.

iPieta—Contains Catholic documents, teachings, writings, prayers, and liturgical calendars. Small fee.

Laudate—Features daily readings, the saint of the day, the Chaplet of Divine Mercy, multiple podcasts for daily meditation, and the *New American Bible*. Free.

Magnificat—Offers prayers inspired by the Liturgy of the Hours, readings, reflections on the daily Mass readings, texts from Church Fathers, and modern spiritual writers. Small fee.

Bible Verses on Giving Thanks

1 Chronicles 16:34

2 Chronicles 5:13

Jeremiah 30:19

Jeremiah 33:11

Isaiah 12:4

Psalm 7:18

Psalm 9:2

Psalm 28:7

Psalm 95:2–3

Psalm 100:4

Psalm 106:1

Psalm 107:8–9

1 Corinthians 1:4–5

2 Corinthians 4:15

2 Corinthians 9:11–12

Ephesians 1:15–16

Philippians 4:6–7

Colossians 3:16–17

1 Timothy 4:4–5

1 Thessalonians 5:18

The *101* Series
from Liguori Publications

College courses numbered 101 usually are intended to give begin-
ners an overview of a topic. The concise books in Liguori Publications' *101* series do just that. Written accessibly by scholars, each
aptly titled book provides information and inspiration on the subject
it covers. Read them and you'll gain a solid foundation about the
Holy Trinity, Jesus Christ, the Holy Spirit, holy Scripture, the Blessed
Virgin Mary, Catholic Church history, Catholic liturgy, the Mass, and
prayer.

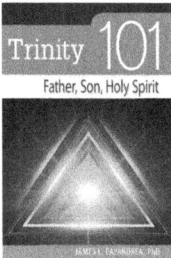

Trinity 101
Father, Son, Holy Spirit
JAMES L. PAPANDREA, PhD

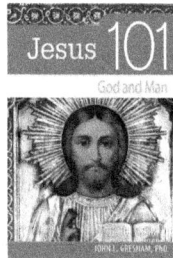

Jesus 101
God and Man
JOHN L. GRESHAM, PhD

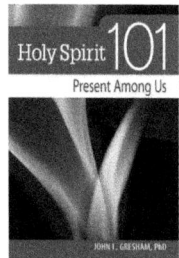

Holy Spirit 101
Present Among Us
JOHN L. GRESHAM, PhD

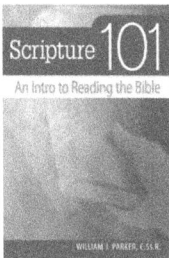

Scripture 101
An Intro to Reading the Bible
WILLIAM J. PARKER, C.SS.R.

Mary 101
Tradition and Influence
MARY ANN ZIMMER, ND, PhD

Church History 101
A Concise Overview
CHRISTOPHER M. BELLITTO

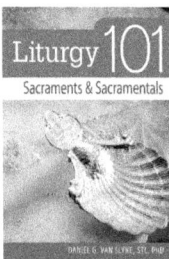

Liturgy 101
Sacraments & Sacramentals
DANIEL G. VAN SLYKE, STL, PhD

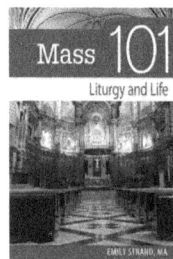

Mass 101
Liturgy and Life
EMILY STRAND, MA

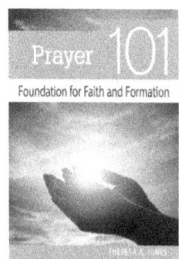

Prayer 101
Foundation for Faith and Formation
THERESA A. RICKARD

Trinity 101:
Father, Son, Holy Spirit
JAMES PAPANDREA, MDIV, PHD
150-page 5.06 x 7.81 paperback
9780764-820823

Jesus 101:
God and Man
144-page 5.125 x 7.375 paperback
819315 / $11.99

Holy Spirit 101:
Present Among Us
JOHN L. GRESHAM, PHD
144-page 5.125 x 7.375 paperback
9780764-819858

Scripture 101:
An Intro to Reading the Bible
WILLIAM J. PARKER, CSSR
144-page 5.125 x 7.375 paperback
9780764-817007

Mary 101:
Tradition and Influence
MARY ANN ZIMMER, ND, PHD
144-page 5.06 x 7.81 paperback
9780764-818516

Church History 101:
A Concise Overview
CHRISTOPHER M. BELLITTO, PHD
144-page 5.06 x 7.81 paperback
9780764-816031

Liturgy 101:
Sacraments and Sacramentals
DANIEL G. VAN SLYKE, STHL, PHD
144-page 5.06 x 7.81 paperback
9780764-818455

Mass 101:
Liturgy and Life
EMILY STRAND, MA
144-page 5.06 x 7.81 paperback
9780764-822254

Prayer 101:
Foundation for Faith
and Formation
THERESA A. JONES, MA
133-page 5.06 x 7.81 paperback
9780764-828591

To order, visit Liguori.org
or call 800-325-9521

Liguori
PUBLICATIONS
A Redemptorist Ministry

www.ingramcontent.com/pod-product-compliance
Lightning Source LLC
La Vergne TN
LVHW051131080426
835510LV00018B/2352